Practical Issues in
Database Management

Practical Issues in Database Management

A Reference for the Thinking Practitioner

Fabian Pascal

ADDISON-WESLEY

Boston • San Francisco • New York • Toronto • Montreal
London • Munich • Paris • Madrid
Capetown • Sydney • Tokyo • Singapore • Mexico City

Many of the designations used by manufacturers and sellers to distinguish their products are claimed as trademarks. Where those designations appear in this book, and we were aware of a trademark claim, the designations have been printed with initial capital letters or in all capitals.

The author and publisher have taken care in the preparation of this book, but make no expressed or implied warranty of any kind and assume no responsibility for errors or omissions. No liability is assumed for incidental or consequential damages in connection with or arising out of the use of the information or programs contained herein.

The publisher offers discounts on this book when ordered in quantity for special sales. For more information, please contact

Pearson Education Corporate Sales Division
One Lake Street
Upper Saddle River, NJ 07458
(800) 382-3419
corpsales@pearsontechgroup.com

Visit AW on the Web: www.awl.com/cseng/

Library of Congress Cataloging-in-Publication Data
Pascal, Fabian.
    Practical issues in database management:
        a reference for the thinking practitioner / Fabian Pascal.
      p. cm.
    Includes bibliographical references and index.
    ISBN 0-201-48555-9
    I. Database management.   I. Title.

  QA76.9.D3 P34855 2000
  005.74—dc21

                                            00-022984

ISBN 0-201-48555-9
Text printed on recycled paper
1 2 3 4 5 6 7 8 9 10—MA—0403020100
First printing, May 2000

A lot of what is being said or written on the subject of database management by vendors, the trade press, and "experts" is irrelevant, misleading, or outright wrong. Although this is true of computing in general, in the database field the lack of knowledge is so acute that, claims to the contrary notwithstanding, technology is actually regressing! This book is dedicated to, and intended for, those who refuse to accept this state of affairs. I also dedicate this book to my father, who did not live to see it.

Contents

Chapter 3

Chapter 4

Chapter 5

The Key, the Whole Key, and Nothing
but the Key: Normalization

Chapter 6

Neither Distinct nor the Same: Entity Supertypes and Subtypes

Foreword

This is Fabian Pascal's third book on database management and it continues in the tradition established by its predecessors. In my foreword to his first book (*SQL and Relational Basics*, M&T Books, 1990) I wrote:

> Relational technology isn't just another way to build a database system; on the contrary, it offers a set of underlying principles that can provide very direct practical benefits to the user (if for no other reason than it enables users to think precisely about the problem they're trying to solve). However, false advertising . . . coupled with the general lack of understanding as to what [those principles] really mean, has had a number of unfortunate consequences: users have been disappointed in their expectations, systems have failed to deliver on the[ir] promise . . . [or] have not been used to their fullest advantage, owing to a lack of appreciation of [those] principles on the part of their users.

Then, in my foreword to Fabian's second book (*Understanding Relational Databases*, John Wiley, 1993), I re-examined the foregoing remarks, asking and attempting to answer the question: Had the situation improved in the past few years? And the answer, sadly, was no it hadn't, at least not by much. Now it seems only appropriate to do the same thing again.

Regrettably, I have to report that matters still don't seem to have improved very much over the past few years. In some respects, in fact, they seem to have deteriorated. A perfect illustration is provided by the SQL standard. Not only is the current version, SQL:1992, seriously deficient in too many ways, but the forthcoming version, SQL:1999, is introducing at least one dreadful new mistake of its own—namely, pointers (!).

SQL deficiencies are, it seems to me, directly due to the widespread lack of understanding (not least on the part of vendors) of fundamental database principles. Certainly it is undeniable that they flout these principles in numerous ways. And the practical consequences are all too obvious: First, users must understand where the deficiencies lie; second, they have to understand just why they *are* deficiencies; third, they have to understand how to work around them; and fourth, they have to devote time and effort in persuading the vendors to remedy them. The trouble is, of course, users too tend to be unaware of those same fundamental principles and, hence, find themselves unable to carry out their side of the "contract" (a "contract" that should not have been allowed or agreed to in the first place, of course). It's a vicious cycle. What is more, this sad state of affairs is not likely to change given the apparent lack of interest on the part of the trade press—itself ignorant of these same principles—in trying to improve matters.

All of which should be more than enough recommendation for you to read Fabian's new book. The aim of this book is to provide a correct and up-to-date understanding of—and appreciation for—the most practical aspects of crucial, yet little understood core database issues. It identifies and clarifies certain fundamental concepts, principles, and techniques that persistently trouble users and vendors. It assesses the treatment of those issues in SQL (both the standard and the commercial implementations) and gives specific guidance and practical advice on how to deal with them (and how not to). It covers, carefully and thoroughly, several particularly tricky and misunderstood topics—complex data types, missing information, data hierarchies, quota queries, and so forth—in a succinct and concise form for the busy database practitioner.

Fabian has been passionately and tirelessly campaigning for many years—certainly ever since I met him in 1986—for users and vendors to educate themselves on fundamentals in order to break the vicious cycle of ignorance and its horrendous consequences. (Parenthetically, I have to say that I admire his persistence; I know only too well what an uphill struggle this business can be.) He is widely known and respected as a writer and consultant on database management, has extensive knowledge of database and SQL technology, and is conversant with the fundamental concepts, principles, and techniques underlying it. He clearly understands the benefits the principles provide and conveys them in an easy-to-understand manner using real-world examples. He is ideally equipped to write a book such as this one.

I wish Fabian success with his new book. Read, enjoy, and pay attention!

C. J. Date
Healdsburg, California, July 1999

Preface

It's official—client server is dead and the future is in the Net.

Says who? Why Larry Ellison, that's who.

"Client Servers were a tremendous mistake. And we are sorry that we sold it to you," the Oracle CEO said to a captive London audience last week.

Instead of applications running on the desktop and data sitting on the server, everything will be Internet based. The only things running on the desktop will be a browser and a word processor.

What people want, he said, is simple, inexpensive hardware that functions as a window on to the Net. The PC was ludicrously complex with stacks of manuals, helplines and IT support needed to make it function. Client server was supposed to alleviate this problem, but it was a step in the wrong direction.

"We are paying through the nose to be ignorant," commented Ellison.
—THE REGISTER (THEREGISTER.CO.UK)

The computer industry—and its database sector in particular—resembles the fashion industry: It is driven by fads. And more often than not, vendors profit from the accelerated obsolescence on which fads are predicated. It's the *users*, however, not the vendors, who pay through the nose. The vendors, helped by the trade media, can profitably exploit ignorance and obscure serious product deficiencies and the questionable practices they induce by simply luring users to the next fad—the Internet being just the latest one.

The Internet is as much a panacea for database management as the PC, SQL, client/server, object orientation, "universal" and multidimensional DBMS, data warehousing, and mining were before it. Java virtual machines, application servers, and browser-based development tools are in the *application,* not database, domain, and problems caused by an unsound database foundation cannot and should not be resolved at the application level. Moreover, ad hoc DBMS support for Web pages, Microsoft Word documents, spreadsheets, and the like— also referred to as "complex data types" and "unstructured data"—adds serious complications and problems of its own (see Appendix 1D for an Internet example). Sound database technology should be a foundation for the Internet, not the other way around. But sadly, the database field is in disarray, if not in outright *regression.*

Many, if not most, difficulties in database management are due to the persistent failure by both DBMS vendors and database users to educate themselves and rely on a sound, scientific foundation in their respective practices. The ad hoc, cookbook approach to database management that results is due in large part to the general business culture, and particularly to the way in which practitioners are introduced to the field. A large majority are self-taught and become DBAs, application developers, database consultants, and even DBMS designers via work with some specific DBMS software. Unexposed to database concepts, principles, and methods, practitioners are unaware of the field's fundamentals, or assume they know them already. But fundamentals are not product- or vendor-specific—and intentionally so: Their generality is precisely what makes them useful. Fundamentals are deemed "theory" and, therefore, not practical. Under industry pressures, even academic programs are becoming increasingly vocational in character, focusing on product *training,* rather than on database *education.* For example:

> **From:** *RA*
> **Subject:** *Database Course*
>
> *We are very interested in additional Oracle instructors . . .*

From: CK
Subject: Database Course

*Does it cover accessing a database via CGI? i.e., VB, Java,
Perl, C++ access to SQL Server or Access DB?*

Yet even a cursory inspection of database practice reveals that most
problems are simply due to lack of database education. Consider, for
example, the following two representative comments, the first a question posed by a novice:

> *I need to store 40 pieces of unrelated information. Is it better to create
> [one] table [with one] record [and] 40 fields, or create [one] table [with]
> 40 records [and one] field?*

The second is a consultant's assessment of a database supposedly constructed by experienced professionals

> *Finished testing a COBOL program for a software company whose main
> product is a well-known government contract accounting system . . . Now
> the [expletive deleted] database . . . is replete with repeating groups,
> redundant fields, etc. On top of all that, because it is one of the central
> files to the entire system, there are literally hundreds of rules and
> relationships, all of which must be enforced by the dozens of
> subprograms that access it. I found so many violations of so many of
> these rules in this new subprogram that I filled five single-spaced pages
> with comments and suggestions. And I probably missed [the more
> obscure problems]. Several [such problems], perhaps.*

The first comment is indicative of how database work is frequently
approached these days; the second shows the severe consequences that
result. It should be obvious that these are *database* (not application)
issues—and *fundamental* issues at that—for the following reasons:

- They underlie *any and all* database projects, regardless of nature
  and purpose.

- No amount of expertise in any DBMS product or platform is sufficient, *in itself*, to address them.

- The consequences of not addressing them are hardly theoretical
  and quite severe.

An analogy can serve to drive the point home. Suppose you were to select a personal physician and there were two candidates: one *educated* in, among other things, anatomy, biology, and chemistry, and one *trained* in a "cookbook" approach to identify symptoms from a list and match treatments from another. Chances are you would opt with the majority for the educated, rather than the cookbook-trained physician, and for a very good reason: In the absence of *knowledge* and *understanding* of health fundamentals, serious problems can be expected. This is generally agreed on in every applied field except, it seems, database management.

The two comments above are not exceptions, but representative of a common, persistent set of problems that keep recurring in database practice. Every chapter of this book starts with some such examples (ironically, a couple are from a review of this book's manuscript). Yet it is almost impossible to make most practitioners pay attention to anything other than product-specific "how-to" recipes, essentially the cookbook approach. Indeed, judging from want ads, the sole technical qualifications for practically all database positions are programming skills and experience with specific DBMS software and development tools on specific platforms (hardware and operating systems). Nothing else. For example:

> **Title:** *Senior Database Architect*
> **Qualifications:** *Minimum of 3 years with Oracle on Solaris. Working knowledge of Tuxedo. Use of database design tools such as ER/Win. Perl and scripting. Familiarity with Oracle 8, Oracle Parallel Server, Sun Clusters, C. At least 3 years of relevant experience.*

> **Title:** *Database Analyst III*
> **Experience:** *Five to nine years developing applications using a major industry-standard relational database system (e.g., Oracle, Sybase, Ingres).*
> **Necessary Skills:** *Oracle DBMS Server and Oracle Application (Web) Server on Windows NT Server; Designer 2000; Developer 2000; Oracle Reports; Oracle Graphics; and PL/SQL. Also a plus: experience with UNIX, VMS, SQR, HTML, JAMA, or JavaScript.*

Is there any wonder then that practitioners, seasoned ones included, have neither a good idea of, nor interest in, database fundamentals? That most cannot offer a useful definition of a database? That DBMS products and databases are riddled with flaws and unnecessary complications, many of which go undetected? If users do not demand sound DBMS products, what incentives do DBMS vendors have to provide them?

Correcting this state of affairs is not a trivial proposition. Because it is easier and more profitable to go with the flow, rather than uphill against it, the vast majority of trade publications, books, and education programs focus almost exclusively on product-specific training and ignore database education, exacerbating rather than solving the problem. On the other hand, the few books that do cover fundamentals have rather tenuous links, if any, to actual database practice, reinforcing the misconception that they are "not practical." Worse, as I have amply demonstrated in other writings, much of what is being written, said, or done about database management is irrelevant, misleading, or outright wrong.

To help break the vicious cycle, this book takes a different approach. It identifies a set of common, recurring database—as distinct from application—issues that users and DBMS vendors (and products) seem to be particularly unclear on, have difficulties with, or fail to address correctly—specifically:

- "Unstructured" data and complex data types
- Business rules and integrity enforcement
- Keys
- Duplicates
- Normalization (and "denormalization")
- Entity subtypes and supertypes

- Data hierarchies and recursive queries

- Redundancy

- Quota queries

- Missing information

A chapter is dedicated to each of these issues, consisting of

- A concise statement of the issue

- A succinct overview of the fundamentals underlying the issue

- A description of the correct and general way of addressing the issue

- A demonstration of the practical benefits of correct treatment and the costs of deviations from, or failure to implement it

- An assessment of whether and how well current technology—SQL and its commercial dialects (and in some cases, proposed alternatives, e.g., object, or "universal" DBMSs)—address the issue

- Recommendations and, wherever possible, workarounds

Organized in this consistent format, the chapters are intended to serve as stand-alone, compact, easy-to-read statements on the current state of knowledge on each issue—"all you need to know" references, so to speak, on subjects most essential to any involvement with databases.

This book has several advantages over the usual fare. First, it is practical not because it ignores or pays lip service to fundamentals like most database books do, but because it demonstrates how *impractical* and costly ignoring the fundamentals is.

Second, many examples are from actual database projects and all chapters include, where pertinent and possible, SQL or product-specific solutions and, when available, workarounds. In addition, each chapter starts with one or more real-world comments like those above, expressing some practical aspect of the issue actually *encountered in practice.* (The identity of the sources is kept anonymous because the purpose is not to single them out, but to demonstrate the scope of the problem.) A good way to read the book is to ponder these comments *before* reading each chapter and try to identify the problems, then revisit them *after* reading the chapter.

Third, the material is intended to be reasonably accessible (though certainly not effortless mentally) to the nontechnical reader, yet useful to the experienced database professional as well. This is because the focus is on *understanding* core aspects of database management, rather than on offering product-specific implementation procedures to be followed on faith. This does not mean that product-specific details are not important, but rather that they are a necessary, but *insufficient* basis for database practice. Sources for product details are in ample supply, but they cannot substitute for understanding database fundamentals—good sources for which are badly lacking.

Fourth, this book is compact. Each chapter covers its issue as thoroughly and succinctly as possible in 15 pages or less. This was no easy feat given the profusion of material on the subject that is scattered throughout disparate sources (Chapter 10 on missing information has 20 references).

As I demonstrated in previous writings (for example, *Understanding Relational Databases,* John Wiley, 1993), database issues are tightly *interdependent.* Thus keys (Chapter 3) are the mechanism for preventing duplicates (Chapter 4), which are one of several types of redundancy (Chapter 8), many of which can be prevented by normalized designs (Chapter 5). Together with keys, data types (Chapter 1) are components of database integrity (Chapter 2), whose enforcement is simplified via normalization (Chapter 5). Therefore, any separation into discrete subjects would be somewhat arbitrary and inhibit understanding. By referencing sources, heavily cross-referencing chapters, and repeating certain essentials in all chapters, the book provides a fifth advantage: It allows readers to focus on the main aspects of each issue by reading only one chapter. They can follow the pointers to related chapters or go to more in-depth sources when necessary.

Sixth, because the content of this book is (intentionally) generic, apart from some illustrative examples, it will not become obsolete like product-specific books do. What is more, it is useful to all practitioners, regardless of which DBMS and what kind of databases they work with, and it enables them to assess pros and cons of their specific circumstances based on general, sound, and objective criteria.

This book can be used for familiarization with and understanding of practical database concepts and principles, as an accessible desk reference, or as a text for teaching purposes (indeed, it was written in part for a database course). On completion, the reader should be able to

- Understand central issues in database management and their practical implications

- Avoid costly misconceptions and fallacies prevalent in the industry

- Appreciate the correct general solutions to core problems

- Assess whether DBMS software offers such solutions

- Overcome, work around, or minimize the consequences if and when products do not offer such solutions

One of the essentials reiterated throughout this book is the definition of a database. Chapter 4 quotes Hugh Darwen as follows:

> A database is a set of axioms. The response to a query is a theorem. The process of deriving the theorem from the axioms is a proof. The proof is made by manipulating symbols according to agreed mathematical rules. The proof [that, is the query result] is *as sound and consistent as the rules are* (emphasis mine).

A DBMS, then, is a deductive logic system: It derives new facts from a set of asserted facts. The derived facts—query results—are true if and only if

- The initial assertions are true

- The derivation rules are (logically) sound and consistent

Database professionals and users desire correct answers from their databases, but a vast majority of them are largely unaware that their practices and the DBMS software they employ fail to adhere to sound and consistent rules. The purpose of this book is to sensitize them to the costly consequences of this state of affairs and to help them minimize the costs as much as is possible.

Fabian Pascal
San Francisco, December 1999

Careful What You Wish For: Data Types and Complexity

The company was using a [SQL] RDBMS . . . to handle data transactions for its trading applications. However, the applications required arbitrary data types, which is nearly impossible for relational systems, according to experts.
—TRADE PUBLICATION ARTICLE

Object-oriented DBMSs . . . support the storage and processing of any type of data, such as text, graphics, diagrams, video, audio, and user-defined data.
—PRODUCT PRESS RELEASE

There is an increasing need of enterprises for complex and function-related data . . . this is [t]he most serious challenge so far . . . to the relational database management system (RDBMS) model, [which] understands only simple types of data . . . [the] solution . . . is arriving in the form of Universal Server[s] . . . RDBMS[s extended with] support for complex data types.
—TRADE PUBLICATION ARTICLE

1.1 The Issue

The data type concept is one of the least understood by database practitioners. This is both a cause and a consequence of the failure by SQL and the commercial DBMSs based on it to implement relational domains, which are nothing but data types whose structure can be as complex as desired. Consequently, blame is being misplaced on the relational approach for the products' lack of support for so-called "complex" types, which permits proponents of the object approach to create an (erroneous) impression that object DBMSs are superior in this respect to relational DBMSs.

This chapter

- Defines and explains the data type concept

- Explains the distinction between "simple" and "complex" types

- Explains what DBMS support of data types means

- Compares the relational and object approaches to data type support

- Discusses implications for database design

- Raises some DBMS design issues

1.2 Fundamentals

Consider a software development company that records information about its employees in its database, for example:

Employee has employee number **100**, *has name* **Spenser**, *works in department* **E21**, *was hired on* **6/19/1980**, *earns a salary of* **$26,150**

Employee has employee number **160,** *has name* **Pianka**, *works in department* **D11**, *was hired on* **10/11/1977**, *earns a salary of* **$27,250**

Expressed in natural language, these are statements of fact or, in logic, propositions about entities of interest (here, employees) asserted to be true. Note that they have the general form

Employee with employee number (**EMP#** *), named (* **ENAME** *), works in department (* **DEPT#** *), was hired on (* **HIREDATE** *), earns a salary of (* **SALARY** *)*

Such generalized forms of proposition are **predicates** in logic, and the terms in parentheses are **value placeholders** (representing entity attributes in the real world). When specific values are substituted for the placeholders, a predicate reduces to an individual proposition, for example, the values

```
{100,Spenser,E21,6/19/1980,26150}
```

reduce the predicate to the first proposition stated above.

For the assertions to be true—that is, facts—the values substituted for the placeholders must be correct in accordance with the business rules in effect at the company (see Chapter 2). **Data types** are, in essence, rules that define, among other things, sets of valid values for a database, constraining the database only to values in those sets. Data types serve as named conceptual pools of permissible values from which actual database values are drawn. Thus, every database value is of a type, or typed.

A data type, or type for short, consists of

- A name
- One or more named **possible representation(s)**, of which
  - One is physically stored
  - At least one is declared to users
- Possible additional **type constraints**
- A set of **operators** permissible on the type's values

Note the critical, but usually missed distinction between a *type* and its *possible representations*—how its values are represented internally in physical storage. A type can have multiple possible representations, for example, a temperature type can be represented internally as degrees Fahrenheit or as hot/warm/cool.

The **actual representation** should be hidden from (invisible to) users for purposes of **data independence**, and they should not need to know anything about it. But at least one representation—the **declared representation**, not necessarily the same as the actual— must be exposed to users by means of operators that can be applied to values represented that way. Values of a type can be manipulated *only* with operators defined for that type. At least one operator must be defined for every type for the user to have access to it: a **specifier** (or **selector**) operator, which specifies (or selects) a value of that type (although more are needed for practicality). Thus, a temperature type can have an actual representation in degrees Fahrenheit, but declare (expose) a hot/warm/cool representation to users. That means that the type would include operators for hot/warm/cool and users would not have to know anything about degrees Fahrenheit; they would simply apply the operators that are provided for the hot/warm/cool values.

Representations, by their very nature, constrain values to specific sets, for example, a Fahrenheit representation constrains temperature values to those on the Fahrenheit scale. But as we shall shortly see, types may (and usually do) impose additional type constraints beyond those inherent in the representations themselves.

Note very carefully that types with different names, operator sets, or type constraints are distinct *even if they have the same representation.* Loosely, distinct types represent different "things" in the real world (e.g., employee numbers, names, department numbers, salaries), and their values are not *meaningfully comparable* even if they "look" the same. It makes no sense, for example, to compare employee numbers to department numbers, even if the values of both are represented as character strings of length 3.

The reader is urged to keep the distinction between type and representations in mind for the rest of the chapter.

1.2.1 "Simple" Types

Two basic types of values are numbers and character strings. They are frequently referred to as **"simple" types** because their values are *perceived* as inherently indivisible or "atomic."

> ❖ **Note:** "Simple" and "complex" (or "unstructured") are terms used informally in the industry that have no precise definitions, hence the quotes.

1.2.2 System-Defined Types

All DBMSs come with one or more built-in **system-defined** variants of the two "simple" types. For example, one product supports the following two types, which represent integers and character strings in the real world:

Type: INTEGER (INT)
Declared representation: INTEGER
Type constraint: >=-231 AND <=231
Operators: set applicable to integers

Type: CHARACTER (CHAR)
Declared representation: CHARACTER
Type constraint: strings of up to 255 characters in length
Operators: set applicable to character strings

The actual (physical) representations of system-defined types are vendor- and/or platform-specific. For example, on Intel computers under Windows NT, this specific product stores values of type INTEGER as 2 bytes and values of type CHARACTER as n bytes, where n is the length of the string. These stored representations are hidden from users (for this reason they are ignored for the rest of this discussion).

Declared representations of system-defined types are usually implicit in the names of the types themselves. For example, type INTEGER's exposed representation is INTEGER (although it does not necessarily have to be), which contributes to the lack of awareness by practitioners of the distinction between a type and its representations and, thus, to the confusion between them.

1.2.3 User-Defined Types

Suppose that the business rule for employee numbers is that they are combinations of one letter and two digits; that is, type EMP# is derived from the more general built-in CHARACTER type as a character string of length 3 with a specific pattern. Note that some of the operators applicable to character strings in general—for example, <, >—would not make sense for EMP# values, even though they may make sense for character strings in general. Thus,

Type: EMP#
Declared representation: CHAR(3)
Type constraint: [A-Z][0-9][0-9]
Operators: set applicable to employee numbers (e.g., selector, =, but
            not <, >)

The EMP# type imposes type constraints—the specific string pattern—in addition to the CHAR representation itself, which constrains EMP# values to character strings of length 3. And its operator set is also different from the set permissible for CHAR.

A possible representation for a SALARY type would be INTEGER with values constrained by a business rule to, say, the 15,000 to 100,000 range. Some of the operators for integers in general, for instance, square root, make no sense for SALARY values. Thus,

Type: SALARY
Declared representation: INT

Type constraint: `=>15000 AND <=100000`
Operators: set applicable to salary values (e.g., selector, =, +, –, <, >,
          but not `SQROOT`)

While these two types have the same representations as the INTEGER
and CHARACTER system types—and are, thus, "simple" too—and their
operators are the same kind of operators, their names and valid value
and operator sets are different. They are, therefore, distinct from the two
system-defined types and only values of the same type can be meaningfully compared. Otherwise put, 'all possible employee numbers' does not
mean the same as 'all character strings of maximum length 255' and 'all
possible employee salaries' is not the same as 'all integers between -231
and 231' (as the particular product defines a built-in INTEGER type).

Unless users can define data types with value and operator sets of their
own choosing, the pools of permissible values and operators for the database will be those built into system-defined types. In this example, the
sets of employee numbers and salaries in the database and the operators applicable to them will be those of the INTEGER and CHARACTER
types, not the ones imposed by the business rules. Furthermore, so will
those of *all* types represented to users as integers or character strings,
even though they have different value, constraint, and operator sets,
therefore, *different meaning.* The DBMS's ability to protect the integrity of
both database content and manipulation would be impaired: It would
have to allow the database values outside the valid sets and blindly execute operations involving erroneous comparisons between, say, EMP#
and DEPT# values.

Obviously, system-defined support for all possible operators for all possible representations of all possible types is not a practical expectation.
Consequently, DBMSs should support **user-defined types** (UDTs) and
operators (sometimes referred to as **user-defined functions** [UDFs],
even though not all such operators are functions). Note very carefully
that, in essence, this means that DBMSs must be *user-extendible.*

1.2.4 Data Type Support

Consider propositions about the company's projects, of the form

*Project (**PROJ#**) has staff size (**STAFF**)*

where STAFF is a data type defined as follows:

Type: STAFF
Declared representation: INTEGER
Type constraint: BETWEEN 0 AND 450
Operators: set applicable to STAFF values (e.g., selector, =, +, −, /)

The operators + and - are meaningful, but how about the / (division) operator? Project staffing ratios may make sense and, if they do, this operator should be available too. But note that its results are of a type different from STAFF, say, S_RATIO with a declared *DECIMAL* representation. Because all values are typed, this type must also be supported by the DBMS with type constraints and operators of its own.

Thus, DBMS support of every operator must include support for types of all possible result values, which, as in this case, may well be distinct types. For n types there are **monadic** (one-operand), **dyadic** (two-operand), **triadic** (three-operand), and so on, up to **n-adic** (n-operand) possible operators and, thus, as many possible result types. DBMS extendibility via UDTs is, therefore, to understate the case, a nontrivial issue for type implementers—be they DBMS vendors or users.

> ❖ **Note:** A fundamental data type that should be universally supported is the **truth-valued type**, whose values are 'true' and 'false'.

1.2.5 On Type "Atomicity"

Consider now a DATE type. One possible representation is CHAR(10).

Type: DATE
Declared representation: CHAR(10)
Type constraint: [Jan,Feb,...,Dec]-[1-31]-[0-...]
Operators: set applicable to date values (e.g., selector, =, <, >, –, but
    not *, /)

Another possible representation is based on three other types—DAY, MONTH, and YEAR, which can be either system- or user-defined as follows:

Type: DAY
Declared representation: INT
Type constraint: INT >=1 AND <=31
Operators: set applicable to days

Type: MONTH
Declared representation: CHAR(3)
Type constraint: [Jan,Feb,...,Dec]
Operators: set applicable to months

Type: YEAR
Declared representation: INT
Type constraint: [0-...]
Operators: set applicable to years

Then the DATE type would be:

Type: DATE
Declared representation: (M MONTH, D DAY, Y YEAR)
Operators: set applicable to dates

This representation has what users perceive as "components" and thus values do not seem as indivisible as in the previous type examples. Nevertheless, DATE values *are* "atomic" *insofar as the DBMS and users are concerned.* Any operators defined for DATE are applied to a *"whole"* DATE value regardless of representation. Take, for example, the HIRE-DATE column in an EMPLOYEES table with values of type DATE. In the first case, where DATE has a CHAR representation, the following

SQL query would apply an equality comparison operator = pertinent to HIREDATE values of the form 'mm-dd-yyy':

```
SELECT *
FROM employees
WHERE hiredate = DATE('Nov-21-1973');
```

In the second case, the following query would apply the = operator pertinent to HIREDATE values of the form ('mm',dd,yyyy):

```
SELECT *
FROM employees
WHERE hiredate = DATE('Nov',21,1973);
```

Even if operators were provided for direct manipulation of the three components themselves, they would not affect the "atomicity" of DATE value. For example, if operators DAY(), MONTH(), and YEAR() were defined to convert values of type DATE to values of types DAY, MONTH, DATE, values would still be "atomic" because such operators would also be applied to "whole" DATE values, presuming nothing about the representation. For example, the query

```
SELECT *
FROM employees
WHERE MONTH(hiredate) = 'Nov';
```

applies the MONTH() and = operators to HIREDATE values of the form ('mm',dd,yyyy), and the user would not have to know anything about the actual representation of DATE and its components. Thus, data types have "atomic" values *by definition*, no matter how complex the representations (this ensures that relational tables are in **First Normal Form** [1NF], [see Chapter 5]).

But note that although the operators in each of the two cases *look* the same as their INTEGER or CHARACTER counterparts, such as =, <, >, they are different—internally their implementation is more complex. In fact, every operator for the first DATE type is also different from its counterpart for the second DATE type. The operator = for DATE with the CHAR(10) representation is internally different from the one for DATE with the component representation.

1.2.6 "Complex" Types

A type, then, is a named set of values without any restriction as to how its values are represented. *Any* representation is acceptable with an arbitrary degree of complexity, including text, images, video clips, sound recordings, geometric forms, maps, and even "arrays of stacks of lists of character strings" [1]. But—and this is the crux of the matter— for users to be able to manipulate their values, *operators must be defined for types with such representations.*

Suppose that the company uses fingerprints for security purposes. There can be a FINGERPRINT type with some form of graphic representation. Propositions about employees would take the general form

> *Employee with employee number (* **EMP#** *) has name (* **ENAME** *), works in department (* **DEPT#** *), was hired on (* **HIREDATE** *), earns a salary of (* **SALARY** *), has a fingerprint (* **EFP** *)*

where EFP is a placeholder for values of type FINGERPRINT, represented as images. There are many possible representations for FINGERPRINT (see Appendix 1A), for example, "two-dimensional arrays of pixels, where each pixel is represented by three numbers designating amounts of red, green, and blue" [2]. A selector and a = operator would have to be defined for this representation, both of which would be invoked whenever a fingerprint—a value (literal) of type FINGERPRINT—is checked against database EFP values of the same type. It should be obvious that these operators would be different and internally would have *more complex* implementations than their counterparts for "simple" types such as INTEGER, CHARACTER, EMP#, SALARY, or even DATE.

And there's the rub, of course: Operators insulate users from representation complexity by "absorbing" or internalizing it. The more complex the representation, the more complex the implementation of the operators. While acceptability of any possible representations "ensures that every value of a type is designatable, such designations might be long-winded when it comes to pictures, videos, sound recordings, engineering drawings, and the like" [3]. In other words, because internally the representations of such types can be quite complex—one reason they are usually referred to as **"complex"** (or **"unstructured"**) **types**—so is the implementation of their operators.

Furthermore, so-called "simple" types, such as INTEGER or CHARACTER, have generally agreed-on operators. Consensus on operators for "complex" types, such as FINGERPRINT, is nowhere near that general. Would users of fingerprints for different purposes, for instance, scientists studying them, agree on what operators, other than the selector and comparison operators, should be defined? How about a PROPERTY type with an image representation: Would users in the real estate business agree on its operators? Or how about a CONTRACT type with text representation: Would the legal profession agree on operators? What about users of these types for different businesses or applications?

The difficulty with so-called "complex" types is that "different instances of [such] data require widely different types of processing [operators], and about the only thing the[se types] have in common is that they are hard to deal with in today's DBMS products" [4]. And the reason for that of course, is not that, as it is frequently claimed, the relational approach cannot "handle complex types"; rather, it is due to the fact that not only is the implementation of operators for such types very complex, but the operators themselves are not even agreed on. For these reasons, "complex" types are better left to type implementers with the necessary expertise in the *application domain* where those types will be used—yet another way of saying that they should be *user-defined extensions to DBMSs* (distinct of *application*). "Complex" types require UDFs, which can be defined for any desired representation and manipulation, but they must be *programmed* into the types to be available to users. This can make things easy for end-users, but quite difficult for type implementers who must program them.

> ❖ **Note:** Appendix 1B illustrates some practical complications raised by the Internet's reliance on "complex" types with representations of the sort listed in Appendix 1A.

1.3 Practical Implications

1.3.1 Relational Domains versus Object Classes

Because the type definition does not place any restriction on type representations, a data model worthy of its name should permit and work with any type, regardless of representation and complexity. In the relational model, this is achieved by the use of **domains**, which are nothing but data types of arbitrary complexity.

In a relational design, predicates map to time-varying tables, placeholders (attributes) map to columns, and propositions map to rows of values drawn from domains. One possible design for the propositions about employees would yield the EMPLOYEES table in Figure 1.1.

The design calls for six user-defined domains (UDTs). Five domains (EMP#, ENAME, DEPT#, HIREDATE, SALARY) are derived from system-defined types, such as INTEGER, CHARACTER, and DATE, and are referred to as "simple." FINGERPRINT is a type usually referred to as "complex" or "unstructured."

An RDBMS that fully and properly supports domains can handle them all. Take, for example, the query "What are the employee number and

EMP#	ENAME	DEPT#	HIREDATE	SALARY	EFP
100	Spenser	E21	06-19-1980	26150	
160	Pianka	D11	10-11-1977	27250	

Figure 1.1. *EMPLOYEES Table*

name of the employee with fingerprint X?" posed by a fingerprint checking operation. It is a relational restrict operation comparing a specific value (literal) of type FINGERPRINT with EFP values of the same type in the database. If the RDBMS supports a user-defined domain FINGERPRINT with the obligatory selector and = operators, this query would work in the same way as a restrict query involving a comparison of values of the "simple" types. For example, using a quasi-SQL dialect

```
SELECT emp#,ename
FROM employees
WHERE efp = [EFPx]
```

where EFP is the column defined over the FINGERPRINT domain, = is a comparison UDF for the domain, and [EFPx] is some (albeit long-winded) denotation of a fingerprint image—a literal (that is, value) of type FINGERPRINT. And this is how all relational operations will work, such as join or intersect, which also rely on the = operator.

Table manipulation in relational databases relies on the operators defined for the database domains. If = operators are defined for "complex" domains (operators that are internally different and more complex than their counterparts for "simple" types), all relational operations (join, difference, and so on) relying on those operators will work with tables containing values drawn from "complex" domains just fine.

The **object class** can be (loosely) considered the object approach's counterpart to the relational domain. Like domains, object classes include **methods**—operators—via which **object class instances**—values—can be manipulated. An object class designer will likely opt for an EMPLOYEE object class, in essence, a data type with a multicomponent representation, where the components EMP#, ENAME, DEPT#, and so on are properties of the class. The class would, therefore, have to include methods that expose those properties to users for manipulation.

> ❖ **Note:** A major problem with object orientation is its fuzziness. One example is the definition of 'object' or 'object class instance': It is not clear whether it is a *value* or a *variable*; depending on context, it is used to mean either and it appears as if it's both.

But as a type, the object class is "the set of all possible employees [and, thus] give . . . no way to hire and fire!" [1]. That is why the relational approach does not have *just* domains (types), but also tables. INSERT and DELETE operations are applied to the tables for hiring and firing. The object approach, on the other hand, lacks a table equivalent to put its class instances (values) in.

> It is odd that so many [object proponents] tend to use employees, departments, and so forth as examples of object classes. An object class is a type, of course, and so those [proponents] are forced to define a "collection" for those employees. What is more, those "collections" typically omit the all-important attribute names, so they are not relational tables. As a consequence, they do not lend themselves very well to the formulation of ad hoc queries, declarative integrity constraints, and so forth—a fact that

advocates of the approach themselves often admit, apparently
without being aware that it is precisely the lack of attribute names
that causes the problems. [1]

In other words, to provide a solution functionally equivalent to the relational one, just object classes and methods are not sufficient; a table equivalent is also necessary. But if it adds tables, the object approach will be no different, in this context, from the relational approach.

A design similar to the relational one but with six object classes is not precluded by the object approach, but a table equivalent would still be needed. On the other hand, the relational approach does not preclude a design with one "complex" EMPLOYEE domain and a one-column table. For querying purposes, the domain would have to include the operators EMP#(), HIREDATE() and so on. Components notwithstanding, because the operators insulate users from the internal structure of the actual representation, the values in the table's one column would be atomic and, therefore, the table would be in first normal form (see Chapter 5) in full relational compliance [1].

1.3.2 Database Design

The discussion in the previous section raises the following issue: Given two design options (a) an EMPLOYEE *type* with a multicomponent representation and a one-column table and (b) a six-column EMPLOYEES table and six domains—how should we choose between them?

> In conventional database design terms, types correspond—
> loosely!—to properties and tables—again loosely—to sets of properties and sets of entities. Hence, if something is "only" a
> property, it should map to a type and not a table. The trouble
> with this idea, of course, is that one person's property is another
> person's entity. [1]

If employees are perceived as *entities*, users will know that entities have properties and what those properties are. As a set of entities and of properties, employees would therefore map to a table, and their properties would correspond to domains. With this design, users will access the properties directly with operators defined for the pertinent domains. For the five "simple" domains, the UDFs will derive from those of the system-defined domains, and only FINGERPRINT will require complex UDFs. If, on the other hand, there is any perception of an employee being a property of some other entity, the property would correspond to a type, and therefore an EMPLOYEE domain would be appropriate. With such a design, users would either not have an interest in the components of the type's representation (employee properties) or, if there were an interest, operators would have to be defined for the components. Note that in either case the domain will require UDFs with more complex derivations than those of the "simple" type operations.

Similarly, fingerprints are likely to be perceived within the company just as a property of employees, which calls for a FINGERPRINT domain with a corresponding EFP column in the EMPLOYEES table. But scientists studying fingerprints may well perceive them as entities with properties of their own, which calls for a FINGERPRINTS table with columns representing those properties and values drawn from respective, likely "simple," domains.

In other words, database design decisions are not scientific, but rather based on subjective perceptions of reality, which may vary across users, or even across purposes and over time for the same user. Different perceptions of reality can lead to either type or table designs even both.

1.3.2.1 Relational Structure versus Object Manipulation

Consider the real case of a company in the business of selling rights to films in various parts of the world. To be able to function, it needs to know, at any point in time, the state of its business. For example, "What rights for what films in what regions have been sold to what customers for what price?" This information is recorded in legal contracts (many of which are generated daily) that spell out the transactions in textual detail. How should the company design its database to answer such queries?

Is a contract a property (type design) or entity (table design)? If a property, a "complex" CONTRACT domain with text representation could be defined. The contracts could be scanned and recorded in the database as "atomic" values of type CONTRACT. Answers to queries such as the aforementioned would require user-defined operators, which, it should be obvious, would be complex (for a sense of such complexity and complications on the Internet, see Appendix 1E). If contracts are entities, the company can structure the informational content of the contracts into a conceptual (business) model consisting of entity types of interest (movies, rights, regions, customers, and so on) with properties of their own. These entity types would map to relational tables with columns defined over mostly "simple" domains, whose operators, like those for EMP# and SALARY, would derive from "simple" system-defined domains.

Either approach produces a database that can, in principle, satisfy the company's needs. A design combining both approaches is also possible with the "complex" CONTRACT type added to the "simple" types, similar to FINGERPRINT. Designs with "complex" types, favored by the object-oriented approach, focus on *manipulation*—operators, methods—as the place to tackle complexity. This shifts the burden to programmers and makes end-users dependent on them (no surprise, given the approach's origins in programming languages). Although the relational approach does not preclude "complex" types, it prefers to tackle at the *structure* (and *integrity*) *level*, shifting the burden to database designers—user parties cognizant of business needs—and minimizing programming. Circumstances like the following are the context in which such design choices must be made.

> *Consider the plight of NASA . . . struggling with . . . how to capture and analyze the [terabytes] of data beamed down to earth daily from orbiting satellites . . . [a] problem is the way in which the raw data must be assigned to tables in order to be processed. This process inherently requires a degree of rationalization and some predisposition toward the ultimate use of the data. This is difficult because the scientist may not know ahead of time what analysis to run on the data. This lack of knowledge severely limits the usefulness of the system.*
> —TRADE PUBLICATION ARTICLE

For any segment of reality, there always exist, in principle, conceptual models mappable to tabular representations, which satisfy given sets of informational needs (as the film company example illustrates). Therefore, "unstructured" data does *not* mean, as is often implied, that information in text or images cannot be represented relationally. It only means that the structuring comes at a price—knowledge, time, and effort. But there is no free lunch—complexity must be tackled somehow. Leaving the information unstructured necessitates complex programming of operators for "complex" types.

Because perceptions are subjective, information structuring is an ad hoc, informal endeavor [5]. If, however, business models are mapped to formal logical representations, then science—logic and mathematics—can be harnessed for managing the data with significant practical benefits. Such mappings are performed by means of a **data model**, which defines the following three properties:

- **Atomicity:** The smallest (indivisible) unit of information
- **Selectivity:** The sensible combinations of units
- **Addressability:** The logical addressing scheme

The relational model is the only known theory-based data model. Based on **first order predicate logic** and **set mathematics**, it defines value as the smallest information unit, the relational operations define selectivity, and the combination (table name + column name + key value) is the addressing scheme.

> ❖ **Note** Whether the object approach has a data model at all is highly questionable, and not only in the sense discussed here [6].

Relational structuring imparts meaning, determining, in essence, the types of questions that can be asked and answered *intelligently*. The practical benefits come from the scientific foundations: correctness, optimizability, data independence, and so on [7].

> The most appropriate design choices will emerge if careful consideration is given to the distinction between (a) declarative sentences in human language and (b) the vocabulary used in the construction of such sentences . . . it is [rows in relational tables] that stand for those sentences, and it is domain values in [columns and rows] that stand for particular elements—typically nouns in that vocabulary. To say it slightly differently: Domains (types) give us values that represent things we might wish to refer to, [relational tables] give us ways of referring to those things in utterances about them. [1]

1.3.3 DBMS Implementation

1.3.3.1 SQL "Domains"

Because no SQL DBMS has implemented domains (on this basis alone—and there are many other grounds—SQL DBMSs cannot be considered truly relational [7]), few practioners know or recall that a relational table's header is not just a set of column names, but actually a set of *column-name/domain-name pairs*. This is at least in part why commercial DBMSs do not provide meaningful support for UDTs.

The SQL standard has a feature called "domain" that allows "primitive (built-in, system-defined) data types names that can be used as short-hand by multiple columns in multiple base table definitions" [8]. For example, assuming a built-in type CHAR, it is possible to create the SQL "domain" EMP#

```
CREATE DOMAIN emp# AS CHAR(3);
```

then use it as a shorthand for CHAR(3) in EMP# column definitions

```
CREATE TABLE employees (emp# emp#, ...);
```

SQL does not support type constraints.

SQL "domains" are not true data types/relational domains. The only domains/data types that the SQL standard does support are the eight system types usually built into commercial DBMSs, "numbers, character strings, bit strings, dates, times, timestamps, year-month intervals, and day-time intervals" [8]. But neither of these types is "complex," which is the main reason for the (erroneous) notion that the relational model "cannot handle complex types." Some products have added support for the storage of IMAGE or TEXT types, but provide practically no operators for them and implementations are proprietary.

> ❖ **Note:** Date, time, and timestamp types were not introduced into ANSI SQL until SQL/92. SQL/99 adds support for the truth-valued domain, but "gets it horribly wrong" [9]. (For practical implications of the lack of support for this domain, see Chapter 10.) Some products allow users to create named rules—a limited form of type constraints—and bind them to columns, but users cannot define their own operators.

Note very carefully that commercial DBMSs do not currently base value comparability on types, but rather on their *representations*. This means that they will actually execute meaningless comparisons if erroneously requested by users and produce results. For example, if the declared representation of both EMP# and DEPT# types is CHAR(3), a SQL DBMS will consider the following query valid, execute it, and produce a result.

```
SELECT *
FROM employees
WHERE emp#=dept#;
```

The correct way to execute this query would be for the DBMS to consider EMP# and DEPT# values to be of distinct types—based on the types' distinct names—and warn the user that the query does not make sense.

1.3.3.2 "Universal" DBMSs

"Universal" DBMSs (UDBMSs) are a recent attempt by SQL DBMS vendors to permit third parties to extend the DBMS with user-defined and "complex" types. As already mentioned, "complex" types tend to be application-specific and their implementation is better left to implementers specialized in the relevant applications. DBMS vendors have neither the knowledge, nor the resources to implement specialized types with complex operators (a cursory inspection of their support of even the "moderately complex" VARCHAR or DATETIME types reveals that implementation is limited, problematic, and proprietary). UDBMSs permit third-party type implementers, or users with the proper expertise in the application domain, to extend the DBMS with their own types.

But driving the support of user-defined "complex" types "deep into the DBMS architecture," as it is sometimes put, raises some nontrivial—to understate the case—issues. With a DBMS extendible by parties other than the DBMS vendor, who is responsible for the following

- Resolution of problems

- Ensuring that DBMS functions, such as integrity enforcement or data independence are not bypassed or violated by the type extensions

- Proper catalog integration of the type extensions

- Performance optimization in processing the user-defined type

Although these issues are intrinsic to all UDFs, for "complex" UDFs they are much more pronounced because of lack of consensus on the operators and the complexity of their implementation. Performance optimization, for example, is a much more acute issue for processing "complex" types with image, sound, or text representations (see Appendix 1C). But this is a *physical implementation* issue on which the data model—which is purely logical—is silent, of course. Should type implementers be allowed to extend and be responsible for the DBMS optimization for their types?

> ❖ **Note** See Appendix 1F for a view that at least a portable alternative to proprietary language extensions may emerge.

1.4 Conclusion and Recommendations

For the reasons discussed in this chapter, DBMS support of "complex" types should not be interpreted as a license for casual deployment of such types, particularly if the purpose is just to avoid data structuring. (Appendix 1D illustrates some of the caveats of Internet reliance on "unstructured" data.) Careful consideration should be given not just to the desirability of the benefits from such deployment, but also to costs, particularly the reliance on programming to develop highly complex specialized operators and the implications of user-extensions to the DBMS. In many circumstances, tackling complexity via "structuring"—database design—can be more cost-effective than programming complex operators because it facilitates reliance on system-defined "simple" types and operators.

Labeling products "universal" or "object oriented" does not magically make complexity or, for that matter, any other fundamental database issues and trade-offs go away. Actually, "universal" is quite misleading because it is the *lack* of universality in processing "complex" data types that causes problems. Moreover, products so labeled tend to add unnecessary complications of their own due to their disregard for the simplicity and reliability of a theoretically sound foundation and their heavy reliance on programming (some object DBMSs are actually "DBMS building kits" of sorts). This explains, in part, the relative low market adoption rate of ODBMS and UDBMS products.

References

[1] C. J. Date and H. Darwen, *Foundation for Object/Relational Databases*, Reading MA: Addison-Wesley, 1998.

[2] H. Darwen, personal communication, 1999.

[3] H. Darwen, personal communication, 1999.

[4] C. J. Date, personal communication, 1999.

[5] F. Pascal, *"Formalizing the Informal,"* Oracle Informant, April 1996.

[6] C. J. Date, "Why the 'Object Model' Is Not a Data Model," *Relational Database Writings 1994–1997*, Reading, MA: Addison-Wesley, 1998.

[7] F. Pascal, *Understanding Relational Databases*, New York, NY: John Wiley & Sons, 1993.

[8] C.J. Date, "SQL Domains Aren't Domains," *Relational Database Writings 1994–1997*, Reading, MA: Addison-Wesley, 1998.

[9] C. J. Date, personal communication, 1999.

1A

Possible Representations for Image Types

File Extension	Representation
AMI	Draw Snapshot (Lotus)
Binary	Group 3 Fax
BMP	Windows or OS/2 bitmap
CDR	Corel Draw Vector
CGM	Computer Graphics Metafile
CMP	LEAD 1-Bit format
CMX	Corel Clip Art Format
CUR	Cursor Format
DCX	(multipage PCX)
DIC	DICOM Format
DRW	MicroGraphx Designer
DXF	(Binary and ASCII) AutoCAD DIF
EPS	Encapsulated PostScript
FMV	FrameMaker
FPX	Kodak FlashPix

File Extension	Representation
GDF	IBM Graphics Data Format
GEM	Graphics Environment Manager Metafile
GIF	Graphics Interchange Format
GP4	Group 4 CALS Format
HPGL	Hewlett Packard Graphics Language
ICO	Icon format
IMG	GEM Paint
JPEG	Joint Photographic Experts Group
MAC	MacPaint
MET	OS/2 PM Metafile
PCD	Kodak Photo CD
PCT	Macintosh PICT Format
PCX	PC Paintbrush
PDF	Adobe Acrobat
Perfect Works	(Draw)
PIC	PC Paintbrush, Lotus picture, Mac PICT drawing
PICT1 & PICT2	(Raster)
PIF	IBM Picture Exchange Format
PNG	Portable Network Graphics Internet Format
PNTNG	MacPaint
PSD	Adobe Photoshop 3.0 bitmap

File Extension	Representation
RND	AutoShade Rendering File Format
SDW	Lotus WordPro graphic file
SRS	Sun Raster File Format
TGA	Targa
TIFF	Tagged-Image File format
TIFF CCITT	Group 3 & 4 Fax Formats
WMF	Windows Metafile
WPG & WPG2	WordPerfect Graphics
XBM	X-Windows Bitmap
XPM	X-Windows Pixmap
XWD	X-Windows Dump

Graphics File Follies

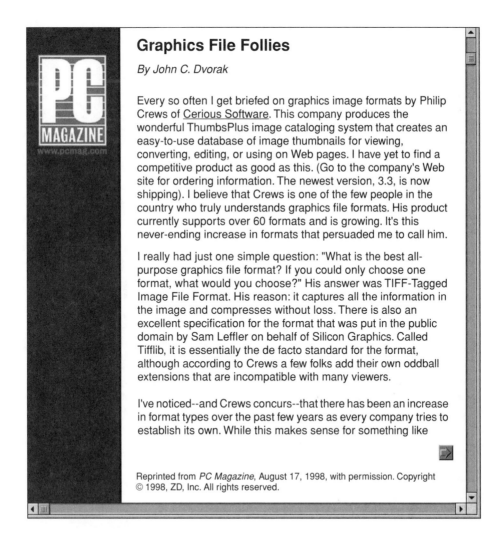

Graphics File Follies

By John C. Dvorak

Every so often I get briefed on graphics image formats by Philip Crews of <u>Cerious Software</u>. This company produces the wonderful ThumbsPlus image cataloging system that creates an easy-to-use database of image thumbnails for viewing, converting, editing, or using on Web pages. I have yet to find a competitive product as good as this. (Go to the company's Web site for ordering information. The newest version, 3.3, is now shipping). I believe that Crews is one of the few people in the country who truly understands graphics file formats. His product currently supports over 60 formats and is growing. It's this never-ending increase in formats that persuaded me to call him.

I really had just one simple question: "What is the best all-purpose graphics file format? If you could only choose one format, what would you choose?" His answer was TIFF-Tagged Image File Format. His reason: it captures all the information in the image and compresses without loss. There is also an excellent specification for the format that was put in the public domain by Sam Leffler on behalf of Silicon Graphics. Called Tifflib, it is essentially the de facto standard for the format, although according to Crews a few folks add their own oddball extensions that are incompatible with many viewers.

I've noticed--and Crews concurs--that there has been an increase in format types over the past few years as every company tries to establish its own. While this makes sense for something like

Adobe Photoshop (which has layer information coded into the PSD format), there's no reason for other companies (such as Corel which used to use TIFF) to develop an in-house format.

Some of the formats are close to idiotic. Have you heard of the KDC format from Kodak, which came in two flavors and is now not even used on some newer cameras? Other formats such as PNG, which was supposed to be a new version of GIF (GIF usage requires a royalty payment to Unisys), have been incorporated into newer browsers, but nobody uses them.

More interesting are two new types of compressed image formats that vie to compete with JPEG. JPEG is the absolute best "free" format for seriously compressing photographic images. Unfortunately, the new compression technologies are all proprietary and require licensing.

According to Crews, these formats will never be widely used, because people who make viewers can't afford to license the technology. Worse, the clueless tightwads who license these technologies won't let Crews do plug-ins. He told me that if he licensed all the oddball formats, it would cost him more than the price of his product ($65). So he came up with the idea of doing plug-ins and just paying for the formats that were sold as plug-ins for the few people who wanted them. "As soon as I came up with that idea, all these guys [with odd formats to license] stopped talking to me," Crews said.

The two new categories of compression are Fractal and Wavelet, both of which can compress further than JPEG, but which require licenses that are out of whack with what Crews considers reasonable pricing. Meanwhile, nobody licenses the new formats.

I would suggest that these compression developers start thinking about two realities. One is that hard disk space is almost free these days, and people don't need compression as much as they used to. Furthermore, the demand for faster online bandwidth will result in higher speeds and will also negate some of the reason that high compression is needed. They should loosen up. Iterated Systems at least allows royalty-free reading (but not writing) of its format, FIF. Of course, this just encourages people to eventually save files as JPEGs.

Unfortunately, according to Crews, the most interesting high-compression methodology is Wavlet which apparently has all sorts of advantages over JPEG and GIF but is simply too pricey to license.

Our discussion eventually turned to the watermarking of images. Crews says that continued manipulation of watermarked images makes it clear that they are subject to damage, no matter what vendors say. Rotation, in particular, takes its toll on the image. Why? Certain low-order bits are changed for the purposes of creating the watermark. This technology stems from a peculiar and seldom discussed encryption technique called steganography, which I find fascinating. Steganography is a process for incorporating data within the image information in much the same way that a watermark is placed within an image. This concept has "spy novel" written all over it. You could theoretically have another picture within the data of a picture. With the right software and password, the second picture could be revealed. Hot stuff.

Our final topic of conversation was the notion of image gamma, a seldom discussed (among PC users) aspect of presentation on a video tube. The default gammas for the Mac and the PC are not the same, and Web sites don't look the same on the two platforms because of it. Nobody seems to understand this important point. The best <u>discussion of gamma</u> can be found on the Web, and everyone should read it because I can't adequately explain the concept in a short column.

The one thing I like about this job of mine is that I have good access to people like Philip Crews. My obligation, of course, is to tell you what I learn. What I learned about graphics file formats is that the situation is getting worse by the minute, and there's no end in sight.

1C

Biometric Tools
Ready to Take Off

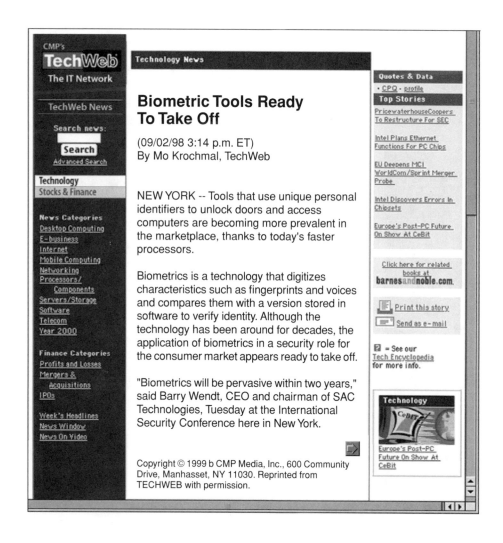

CMP's TechWeb
The IT Network

Technology News

TechWeb News

Search news:

[Search]

Advanced Search

Technology
Stocks & Finance

News Categories
Desktop Computing
E-business
Internet
Mobile Computing
Networking
Processors/
    Components
Servers/Storage
Software
Telecom
Year 2000

Finance Categories
Profits and Losses
Mergers &
    Acquisitions
IPOs

Week's Headlines
News Window
News On Video

Biometric Tools Ready To Take Off

(09/02/98 3:14 p.m. ET)
By Mo Krochmal, TechWeb

NEW YORK -- Tools that use unique personal identifiers to unlock doors and access computers are becoming more prevalent in the marketplace, thanks to today's faster processors.

Biometrics is a technology that digitizes characteristics such as fingerprints and voices and compares them with a version stored in software to verify identity. Although the technology has been around for decades, the application of biometrics in a security role for the consumer market appears ready to take off.

"Biometrics will be pervasive within two years," said Barry Wendt, CEO and chairman of SAC Technologies, Tuesday at the International Security Conference here in New York.

Copyright © 1999 b CMP Media, Inc., 600 Community Drive, Manhasset, NY 11030. Reprinted from TECHWEB with permission.

Quotes & Data
• CPQ - profile

Top Stories
PricewaterhouseCoopers To Restructure For SEC

Intel Plans Ethernet Functions For PC Chips

EU Deepens MCI WorldCom/Sprint Merger Probe

Intel Discovers Errors In Chipsets

Europe's Post-PC Future On Show At CeBit

Click here for related books at
barnesandnoble.com.

Print this story
Send as e-mail

= See our
Tech Encyclopedia
for more info.

Technology
Europe's Post-PC Future On Show At CeBit

Szulik comments on Linux and competition from Microsoft's Windows 2000.

The growing market is a direct result of today's advanced computer hardware. The faster, cheaper PCs on the market can handle the data processing needed to verify an identity from a fingerprint, a voice, or a face -- all in the time it would take to swipe a card or type in a password.

"You need processing power to do this in real time," Wendt said.

While the biometric industry is producing iris scanners, thermal face and hand scanners, and other high-tech mechanisms, the leading biometric tools incorporate simpler fingerprint, facial, and voice verification, he said.

Fingerprint recognition has a long history of use in law enforcement and it can be computerized fairly cheaply, for less than $50, Wendt said. Houston-based Compaq is offering a $99 fingerprint reader as a peripheral for its Deskpro line and has licensed biometric software.

Voice-recognition technology doesn't take much to build, Wendt said. "A little software, some hardware, 8-bit digitization, a $1.50 microphone, and you have some pretty discriminating technology," he said. "Facial-verification technology can be implemented for less than $50."

In Las Vegas, casinos are already using facial verification to identify people and keep out undesirables, Wendt said. "They can verify your identity even if you have your hand over your mouth," he said.

"Voice-verification technology -- like all biometrics -- is not a silver bullet, but it works quite well," said Robert Doherty, business-development manager for Keyware Technologies, a biometric company based in Woburn, Mass. For verification, Doherty said, a scan simply has to fall within a reasonable range in the software template.

For mass-market use, this kind of technology has to be nonintrusive and fast, Wendt said. "The technology has to be transparent -- you can't ask people to do something different than what they are already doing," he said.

1D

Search Engine Failures

Search Engine Failures

By John Dvorak, PC Magazine
October 20, 1998 9:42 AM PT

www.pcmag.com

One of the Web's biggest disappointments is the faded promise of search engine technology. None of the engines (or even the directories) work as advertised. When given a quality query, search engines return spotty and inconsistent (if not pathetic) results. Even worse, there's an element bordering on fraud regarding the "submit your site to us" malarkey that all of the engines and sites promote. I say this because I've made various sites for the sole purpose of testing these mechanisms, and not once was I successful. Furthermore, those automated software submission programs don't seem to work either.

Let's start with the simple John C. Dvorak Web site at www.dvorak.org. Many people don't realize that if you simply type something at the top of the browser in the URL field, such as Dvorak, the browser will look for any number of possible sites incorporating the name. Try it. Most often you'll actually arrive at the Dvorak.org site. You'd think that if you put something more specific (such as John C. Dvorak) into a search engine that it would find the Dvorak.org site, wouldn't you? Especially since I've submitted the site over and over for over a year to all the engines.

So what do you get? Well, with AltaVista I get these returns:

1-2: Links to bootleg copies of an old column I wrote in 1991!
3: A 1996 MacUser column.

4: A PC Magazine column in Polish.
5: A PC Magazine column in Norwegian.
6: An out-of-date biography.
7: Yet another copy of the bootleg column.
8-10: The exact same 1996 PC Magazine Online column that seems to be the only one ever found by any search engine, despite nearly 200 columns for PC Magazine Online. This same column (called "No Cameras Allowed") shows up so often that it mystifies me.

Dvorak.org does appear as number 11, and I consider this to be something of a miracle.

My current favorite search engine is Inference Find, which consolidates information from various other engines, but it's suddenly lost the ability to find Dvorak.org, even though it shows up as number 11 on AltaVista.

Instead, I get numerous references to the Dvorak keyboard and even to Joe Dvorak's home page. I'm reconsidering Inference Find as a favorite, since it's getting worse, not better.

At Yahoo!, my Dvorak.org site appears as number two, making me wonder what exactly is happening at Inference. The number one hit for John C. Dvorak at Yahoo! is the Scott St. John Home Page, and the number three hit is for Sutton Place Gourmet, a recipe site that has no reference to a John, a "C," or a Dvorak. Does this kind of mistake bother anyone at the search companies?

HotBot is no stranger to search deterioration. John C. Dvorak comes back with a "too many hits" error, and when you change the criteria by clicking on the person option, it gets down to 2,200 hits. But what kind of hits? The first one (99 percent relevance) is a column by John E. Dvorak, who happens to write about marijuana issues. Then hits two through eight are exactly the same: each references a PC Magazine column called "The End is Near." That's followed by two more duplicates. Most of the hits are random, and I never did find Dvorak.org on HotBot.

Lycos finds the Dvorak.org site on page three and keeps suggesting that I try HotBot, but at least it manages to get the job done.

<u>Excite</u> is all over the map and never finds the site. Worse, it kept feeding me advertisements for Music Boulevard and Antonin Dvorak music disks in particular.

Talk about over-targeted advertisements. This is particularly galling, because it appears that more effort is being put into spamming you with targeted ads than into making the engine work! What are the priorities here? Obviously not to serve the user. Excite is pathetic. At the bottom, the page asks me if I want to use WebCrawler. Maybe it knows something that I don't know. So I try it.

In fact, <u>WebCrawler</u> is worse. This engine hasn't done squat for years. The number one hit is for John N. Dvorak, and then it lists one column by me and 20 or more sites about the Dvorak keyboard. Instead of finding Dvorak.org (which I submitted to the site over a year ago), it finds the home page of Joe Dvorak (who is this guy?). This engine is just plain useless.

So I then go to <u>Ask Jeeves</u>, a site which people keep telling me to put on my <u>Universal Home Page</u>. I find it to be gimmicky and useless. At this site, you ask questions. OK, I ask "Who is John C. Dvorak?" Simple enough. Too bad it comes back with two boxes asking me if I want to find out more about Antonin Dvorak, one box about the Dvorak keyboard, and one box for Radek Dvorak. It also reiterates the bad hits found elsewhere and tells me that AltaVista actually found seven exact hits on that bootleg column I complained about earlier. Totally useless.

Rather than Ask Jeeves, I use <u>Dogpile</u> for this kind of shotgun search. It goes from engine to engine, using a lot of obscure ones to find your target. In this case, it comes back with a search done by <u>Thunderstone</u>, which hits Dvorak.org on number three. Unfortunately everything else on the list is random or very obscure (which is good, too). Thunderstone found at least a dozen references I was unaware of.

Playing with Thunderstone, I'm reminded of my first look at HotBot back when it was fresh and good. I wonder if all search engines just deteriorate over time. Maybe they need to erase everything and start over. There's a good chance I'll be complaining more about this problem in the weeks ahead, so brace yourself.

1E

"Complex" Types and Operators: An Internet Illustration

DB2 magazine

DB2 is a registered trademark of IBM and is used here under Licence

db2mag.com

Resources

Archives

Advertise

Write for Us

Contacts

Subscribe

Tell us
What you Think

What is XML?

Why XML?

DB2's XML support

New XML support and the DB2 XML Extender will give DB2 a whole new range of e-commerce and Web-publishing possibilities.

PLUGGING IN to XML

by Harold Treat

WHAT IS XML?

XML is a text-based document formatting language. The term XML is often used to refer to a collection of related specifications including Extensible Style Language (XSL), XML Linking Language (XLink), XML Pointer Language (Xpointer), and Document Object Model (DOM).

XML syntax is implemented as a set of tags used to mark up a document. Although it's similar in style to HyperText Markup Language (HTML), XML allows content authors to extend the language by defining their own custom tags. This feature makes XML a meta-language, meaning that it can be used to define markup languages, or grammars, specialized to the needs of a company, industry, or discipline that can be read by any XML-enabled system.

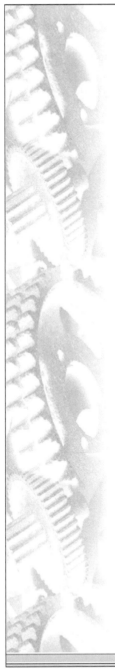

HTML tags are meant for Web browsing; they enable interaction between humans and computers. To understand the differences between HTML and XML, consider these examples.

```
<p><b>Mrs. Mary McGoon</b> <br>
1401 Main Street <br>
Anytown, NC 34829
</p>
```

If you're familiar with HTML, you know that this code looks something like this when rendered by a browser:

Mrs. Mary McGoon
1401 Main Street
Anytown, NC 34829

The HTML tags don't contain any information about what the data is; they only describe how it should look. If you want to extract the ZIP code from this address, you could write an algorithm like this:

Look for a paragraph tag that contains text in boldface, followed immediately by two text strings preceded by a break tag. In the text following the second break tag, assume everything up to the comma is the name of the city; it will be followed by two tokens, the second of which is the ZIP code.

While this algorithm works for this HTML sample, it's easy to think of perfectly valid addresses that break this algorithm.

1F

Java and Database Synergy

> ❖ **Note:** The views expressed are the author's own. It is emphasized that wherever possible, declarative solutions are always preferable to procedural ones, and this is not negated by the availability of better, more portable procedural languages, which, of course, are desirable.

The main SQL DBMSs are supporting Java by embedding a Java Virtual Machine (JVM) in their server versions. This shotgun marriage is the beginning of a potential new synergy—a combination of relational database and object-oriented capabilities.

With support from the major vendors, Java is available for most DBMSs. Developers now have a stored procedure language that can be portable across different products. Java provides a viable alternative to the vendors' proprietary stored procedure languages.

However, Java is more than just a portable stored procedure language. Java objects can be stored as values in database columns. These are special columns whose type is a Java class. Java column values are active objects whose methods can be accessed in SQL commands or when retrieved locally.

In the absence of standard specifications, stored and triggered procedure languages have usually been proprietary to each DBMS. Using portable programming languages like C++ for database stored procedures has raised issues of safety (an errant procedure could crash the server) and security. Now, with most vendors supporting it, Java can become the stored procedure language of choice, promising portability and safety.

Java servlets are an excellent fit as a stored procedure language:

- *Portability.* Java database servlets can be written in Pure Java using standard JDBC for database access.

- *Safety.* Java code is free from pointer misuse and memory leaks. The JVM applies the sandbox approach to executing Java code, restricting external access.

- *Security.* The JVM sandbox mechanism provides secure execution of Java code. The JVM also supports authentication of Java servlets.

With a portable stored procedure language, code can be transferred between different DBMSs, vendor-specific training is reduced, and database-independent applications can be distributed with application-specific stored procedure code.

Even more revolutionary than Java database servlets is the ability to define the type (domain) of a database column as a Java class. The major commercial DBMSs support cataloging Java classes in the database. Columns in database tables can then use the class for their domain definition.

In the rows of database tables, the value of a column defined over a Java class is an object instance of the Java class. Instances are created using the constructor for the class. Column values are active instances. Their methods are callable in SQL commands. When the client retrieves a column value defined as a Java class, it is an active object that is often executed in the client's JVM. Both class and instance methods may be accessible.

Java objects in SQL databases are a good synergy of object-oriented programming and relational databases. They greatly extend the expressive power of SQL, while making object-orientation techniques available to database developers.

How should relational databases and object-oriented programming be combined using Java? The major vendors have opted for embedding Java in their DBMSs by including a JVM in them. The server embedded JVMs are all proprietary. This is because the JVM must be tightly integrated with the database system. Special internal interfaces are required because the main server is implemented in a different language (usually C/C++).

Are the proprietary JVMs going to do the job? Or are they replacing proprietary stored procedure languages with an only somewhat more portable language? Compatibility and efficiency will be a problem. Will the database Java dialects be able to keep up with enhancements in the language and improvements in JVM technology? The JVMs from database vendors will hardly be best-of-breed.

One consideration is compatibility between the JVM running on the database server and any JVM running on the client system. This is needed to retrieve Java objects from the database and efficiently execute them on the client. To achieve compatibility, the client may need to use a database vendor supplied or recommended JVM.

There is a more effective solution: DBMSs implemented entirely in pure Java with both the DBMS on the server and any Java servlets or database objects running on the same JVM. Database administrators can choose the best JVM for their server configuration. They can select the JVM for the client from a wide variety of vendors to meet the desired compatibility. Execution of user-defined Java servlets and database objects is more efficient with a Java RDBMS because no translation bridges to the DBMS are required. There is also a severe reduction in memory overhead, as the RDBMS uses native JVM services.

Lee Fesperman
CEO, FFE Software
(www.firstsql.com)

2

The Rule of Rules: Integrity

[U]nless you have a penchant for walking close to the edge, you should make sure that . . . application[s] enforce . . . integrity.
—TRADE PUBLICATION ARTICLE

In the short term you have two options (a) disable referential integrity checking and make the change (not recommended unless you're willing to assume total responsibility for the data consistency checking yourself; and you have to ensure you have exclusive access to the DB when you're doing this); (b) use our triggers and stored procedures to implement the RI procedurally.
—DBMS VENDOR ADVICE

Finished testing a COBOL program for a software company whose main product is a well-known government contract accounting system . . . Now the [expletive deleted] database . . . is replete with repeating groups, redundant fields, etc. On top of all that, because it is one of the central files to the entire system, there are literally hundreds of rules and relationships, all of which must be enforced by the dozens of subprograms that access it. I found so many violations of so many of these rules in this new subprogram that I filled five single-spaced pages with comments and suggestions. And I probably missed [the more obscure problems]. Several [such problems], perhaps.
—ONLINE MESSAGE

2.1 The Issue

There is a lot of talk about business rules these days. Unfortunately, much of it reflects a very poor understanding of the implications for database integrity enforcement—a critical, if not arguably, the most critical—aspect of database management. Indeed, not only can integrity take as high as 70% to 80% of the system development and maintenance effort, but any failure in this regard can result in corrupt databases, rendering the whole effort useless, even dangerous. But in the absence of proper understanding, integrity has been weakly addressed by DBMS vendors, with quite costly and possibly insidious consequences.

This chapter

- Explains the concepts of business rule, integrity constraint, and integrity rule, and the distinctions between them

- Provides a classification scheme for integrity rules and examples for four rule categories

- Explains the concept of constraint inheritance by derived tables

- Clarifies the DBMS integrity enforcement mechanism and the important distinction between declarative and procedural integrity support

- Discusses and assesses the integrity support available in SQL and its commercially implemented dialects

- Concludes with some practical recommendations

2.2 Fundamentals

Databases are *structured* collections of facts or, more precisely, represent propositions—assertions of fact purported to be true. Consider a hotel reservations database, which records propositions of the following general form

> *Reservation identified by reservation number (**RES#**), made for room with number (**ROOM**), has scheduled arrival date (**ARR_DATE**), has scheduled departure date (**DPT_DATE**)*

Formally, this generalized form of proposition is a **predicate**, and the terms in parentheses are **value placeholders**. Substituting specific values for the placeholders yields propositions about specific reservations. For example, the values

{990000,333,7/26/1995,7/28/1995}

yield the proposition

> *Reservation identified by reservation number* **99000** *for room* **333** *had arrival date* **7/26/1995** *and scheduled departure date* **7/28/1995**

Propositions are represented in the database by rows in tables—sets of values—which, when substituted for the placeholders in the predicate, yield those propositions. Figure 2.1 shows the reservations table RESERVE, where the displayed row represents the specific proposition listed just previously (informally, reservations are the entities of interest; columns represent entity attributes).

❖ **Note:** The table has two composite natural candidate keys {ROOM#,ARR_DATE} and {ROOM#,DPT_DATE}. There is no objective criterion on the basis of which either should be preferred as the primary key for referential purposes. It is advisable in such cases to define a simple surrogate key, such as RES#, the common practice for reservation systems (see Chapter 3).

RES#	ROOM	ARR_DATE	DPT_DATE
99000	333	07/26/1995	07/28/1995
89000	300	07/23/1995	07/25/1995

RESERVE

Figure 2.1. *RESERVE Reservations Table*

The propositions represented in the database must be true; otherwise the database would represent falsehoods, not facts. The truth of the represented propositions and, thus, the correctness of database representation, depends on whether the row values representing them are *(a)* consistent with the business rules in effect and *(b)* physically correct (that is, they are not erroneous).

> ❖ **Note:** The distinction between *(a)* and *(b)* is important. For example, it is entirely possible to have a scheduled departure date that is perfectly acceptable as such, but is not physically correct in the sense that it is not the one actually specified by the customer—for example, a data entry error. It's only when values fall outside the valid set imposed by business rules in effect that they can be rejected by DBMS, as it cannot know when *valid* values are erroneous.

2.2.1 Business Rules

Suppose a hotel opened on 1/10/1980, has 350 rooms, and books up to 100,000 reservations per year. Some of the business rules are

R1: *Reservation numbers are between 1 and 100000*

R2: *Room numbers are between 1 and 350*

R3: *All arrivals are later than 1/10/1980*

R4: *For all reservations, scheduled departure is later than arrival*

R5: *Reservations have distinct reservation numbers*

R6: *For every reservation, the combination of room number and arrival date is unique*

R7: *For every reservation, the combination of room number and scheduled departure date is unique*

R8: *Reservations for the same room do not overlap*

Business rules, like propositions and predicates, are expressed in real-world terms: rooms, reservations, arrivals, and departures.

2.2.2 Integrity Constraints

In the same manner in which propositions about the real world are represented in the database by table rows, business rules in the real world are represented in the database by **integrity constraints**, which are business rules translated into database terms—tables, columns, and rows. In other words, integrity constraints are to business rules what rows are to propositions; they are an integral part of the **logical model** [1]. Their name derives from their function, which is to constrain database values to only those that yield rows representing true propositions (facts).

Constraints can be of arbitrary complexity and are classified in four categories [2].

2.2.2.1 Domain Constraints

Domains (data types) are named pools of values from which the values populating the database tables are drawn. They consist of at least one possible value representation, a permissible value set, and an applicable operator set (see Chapter 1).

The constraints representing business rules R1, R2, and R3 are **domain constraints**, namely

    D1: DOMAIN res# INTEGER(5) > 0 AND <= 100000

    D2: DOMAIN room INTEGER(3) >= 1 AND <= 350

    D3: DOMAIN res_date DATE >= 1/10/1980

where RES#, ROOM, and RES_DATE are domain names.

2.2.2.2 Column Constraints

Database columns, representing real-world attributes, draw their values from the value sets defined by domains (see Chapter 1). A **column constraint** specifies the domain over which a column is defined, thus restricting its values to just those within the domain set.

The ARR_DATE and DPT_DATE columns are both defined over the RES_DATE domain. Similarly, the ROOM and RES# columns draw their values from the RES# and ROOM domains, respectively. The column constraints for the RESERVE table are

C1: `reserve.res# DOMAIN res#`

C2: `reserve.room DOMAIN room`

C3: `reserve.arr_date DOMAIN res_date`

C4: `reserve.dpt_date DOMAIN res_date`

2.2.2.3 Table Constraints

Table constraints are integrity constraints that are neither domain nor column constraints and apply to one table. There are **single-row** and **multirow** table constraints.

The table constraint representing business rule R4 is single-row:

T1: `reserve.dpt_date >= reserve.arr_date`

Examples of multirow table constraints are those representing rules R5, R6, and R7. Such uniqueness constraints are known as **key constraints** (see Chapter 3). R5 is represented by a primary key constraint

T2: `reserve.res# PRIMARY KEY`

Rules R6 and R7 are represented by candidate key constraints (see Chapter 3).

```
T3:   reserve.(room,arr_date) UNIQUE
```

```
T4:   reserve.(room,dpt_date) UNIQUE
```

The multirow constraint representing rule R8 is more complex

```
T5:   r2.res# <> r1.res#
      AND r2.room = r1.room
      AND r2.arr_date < r1.dpt_date
      AND r2.dpt_date > r1.arr_date
```

> ❖ **Note:** The long form of the constraint is "There should not be any two rows r1 and r2 with the same ROOM value such that the ARR_DATE value in r2 is less than or equal to the ARR_DATE value in r1, or the DPT_DATE value in r2 is greater than or equal to the ARR_DATE value in r1." T5 is a more succinct, less verbose formulation, derived as follows:
>
>
> t1 is the time interval between the arrival date A1 and the departure date D1 of reservation R1. The interval t2 of another reservation R2 of the same room does not overlap that of R1, +1 if its departure date D2 is earlier than, or on A1 (case T2'), or its arrival date A2 is later than, or on D1 (case T2").
>
> Thus, for any two distinct reservations R1 and R2 of the same room, the *no-overlap* condition is
>
> D2 <= A1 OR A2>= D1
>
> or, expressed negatively, the *overlap* condition prohibited by the rule is
>
> NOT (D2 > A1 AND A2 < D1)

2.2.2.4 Database Constraints

Database constraints span two or more tables.

A well-known example is the **referential integrity** constraint, constraining foreign key values to match values of the primary keys they reference (see Chapter 3). Assuming the table

```
CUSTOMERS {CUST#,NAME,RES#,...}
```

where RES# is a foreign key referencing the primary key in the RESERVE table, the referential constraint

```
FORALL customers (EXISTS reserve
(reserve.res# = customers.res#))
```

is a database constraint which can be expressed in shorthand as

```
    DB1: customers.res# FOREIGN KEY
         REFERENCES reserve.res#
```

2.2.3 Database Correctness

As already mentioned, the meaning of a time-varying database table is its predicate. A table represents the real world correctly *if and only if,* for every row, when all values are substituted for the respective placeholders in the predicate, the predicate evaluates to true. Thus "the predicate for a given [time-varying table] represents the **criterion for update acceptability** for that [table]—that is, it constitutes the criterion for deciding whether or not some proposed update is in fact valid (or at least plausible) for the given [table]" [3]. This is a formal way of ensuring that all rows represent true propositions and, thus, the table is a correct representation of the real world.

For practical reasons it is very desirable that the DBMS—not users in applications—ensure that no database row represents a false proposition [1]. But "in order for it to be able to decide whether or not a proposed update is acceptable for a given [table], the DBMS needs to be aware of the predicate of that [table]" [3]. Note, though, that the DBMS has no way of knowing which values make a predicate evaluate to true or false. Neither can it understand what certain terms in predicates mean, for example, 'identified by', 'made for', and 'had' in the reservation predicate

*Reservation identified by reservation number (**RES#**), made for room with number (**ROOM**), had arrival date (**ARR_DATE**), had departure date (**DPT_DATE**)*

This is why such terms are not recorded in the database. What the DBMS can know is that any row with any value that violates any of the integrity constraints declared for the table—and, thus, violates the business rules in effect—cannot possibly represent true propositions. "Formally, therefore, we can define the (DBMS-understood) 'meaning' of a given base [table] to be the logical *and* of all column and [table] constraints that apply to that base [table] (and it's the meaning that the DBMS will check whenever an update is attempted on the base [table] in question)" [3]. In other words, the least and the best the DBMS can do to ensure table correctness is to enforce all column and table integrity constraints declared for each table. The constraints serve as the best approximation of the table predicate and can, therefore, be used by the DBMS as the criterion for update acceptability for each table. By extension, the **database predicate**—the meaning of the whole database—is all table predicates (domain, column, and table constraints) ORed together and ANDed with all database constraints [3].

The sum total of the integrity constraints on the RESERVE table, for example, is thus

```
reserve.res# DOMAIN res#
OR
reserve.room DOMAIN room
OR
reserve.arr_date DOMAIN res_date
```

```
OR
reserve.dpt_date DOMAIN res_date
OR
reserve.res# PRIMARY KEY
OR
reserve.dpt_date => reserve.arr_date
AND
r2.res# <> r1.res#
AND r2.room = r1.room
AND r2.arr_date < r1.dpt_date
AND r2.dpt_date > r1.arr_date
```

If the DBMS knows and understands these constraints, it can check every row that is a candidate for insertion in the database against them and take proper action if it detects any violation. For example, the row

```
{99000,333,07/26/1995,07/28/1995}
```

yields the true proposition

> *Reservation identified by reservation number **99000**, made for room **333**, had arrival date **07/26/1995**, had scheduled departure date **07/28/1995***

because its values do not violate any of the column and table constraints on RESERVE. It should be allowed into the database. On the other hand, the row

```
{99000,360,07/26/1995,07/28/1995}
```

yields a false proposition because the value '360' violates the column constraint imposed by the ROOM domain on the ROOM column: The value is outside the domain range of 0 to 350. This row should not be permitted into the database.

2.2.4 Base versus Derived Constraints

Constraints on base tables are declared by users. Derived tables, such as views, on the other hand, *inherit* their constraints from the base tables over which they are defined [1]. If the DBMS is to know the constraints on derived tables, it needs

> a set of rules such that if the DBMS knows the [integrity constraints] for the input [base tables] and relational operators [that define the view], it can deduce the [integrity constraints] for the output from that operation [the view] . . . the rules follow immediately from the definition of the relational operators. For example, if A and B are any two type-compatible tables and their respective [applicable sets of integrity constraints] are PA and PB, then the [set of constraints] PC for [view] C, where C is defined as A INTERSECT B, is obviously (PA) AND (PB); that is, a row r [should be allowed] in [view C] if and only if [it is a valid row of base tables] A and B. [3]

And so on for all other table operators, such as join, union, and difference. In other words, correct view updates are predicated on the DBMS's ability to *infer* a view's set of integrity constraints from those on the base table(s) over which the view is defined and the table operation by which it is derived. A properly designed relational DBMS would make such inferences for views and enforce the derived constraints, such that view updates propagate correctly to the underlying base tables [4, 5].

❖ **Note:** If there are *cross-table duplicates* (that is, tables with overlapping predicates), the results of some view updates may seem "surprising" or "arguably counterintuitive" even if logically correct, for example, an INSERT into a view resulting in INSERTs into multiple base tables. The consequences of cross-duplication are much more serious if the DBMS does *not* make constraint inferences because then it cannot guarantee correct propagation of view updates to the underlying base tables and may leave the database in an inconsistent state. For these reasons database design should adhere to the **principle of orthogonal design** [3], which prohibits the duplication of whole rows or parts thereof across tables (see Chapter 8).

2.2.5 Integrity Enforcement

Integrity enforcement for every update operation, then, involves *(a)* the DBMS checking, for every update operation, a table's *after-update* state against the constraints applicable to the table, and, if a violation is discerned *(b)* a DBMS response to prevent it. To enforce the no-overlap constraint on RESERVE, for example, the DBMS must compare every row in the after-update state of RESERVE to all its other rows (which amounts, loosely, to performing a self-join) and rejecting any offending row(s). Thus, checks for table integrity constraints are essentially table operations performed by the DBMS. The self-join in the no-overlap case involves checking multiple rows in a single table, which is the case for a multirow table constraint.

❖ **Note:** For simplicity, the term "table" (**relation**) is used throughout this book for what are actually *time-varying* tables (**relation variables**, or relvars for short). A table's body of rows varies over time via updates, so a table at any point in time is a snapshot [6], a value of a relvar. A table update operation can be viewed as a replacement of the whole table (set of rows) with a new one. For example, the insertion of three new rows in a 1,000-row table can be seen as replacing it as a whole with 1,003 new rows, 1,000 of which happen to be identical to the previous ones. In other words, the after-insert table is equivalent to the union of the before-insert table and the newly inserted rows. Update and delete operations can be viewed the same way.

2.2.5.1 Integrity Rules

Integrity rules are the DBMS constraint enforcement mechanism [1]. They consist of

- A name, for example, R8

- An integrity constraint, for example, no-overlap (T5)

- A **checking time** (immediate or deferred)

- A **violation response** (rejection or compensating action) [7]

> ❖ **Note:** The terms "business rule," "integrity constraint," and "integrity rule" are often used interchangeably, but they are distinct and should not be confused. Business rules, such as R1 to R6, are part of the conceptual (business) model and are expressed in real-world terms (reservations, rooms, customers). Integrity constraints, such as D1 to D3, C1 to C3, T1 to T3, and DB1, are part of the logical model and are expressed in database terms (tables, columns, rows). Integrity rules are also expressed in database terms, but they include a checking time and violation response in addition to the constraint. For the majority of constraints, checking is immediate and the response is rejection.

The last three rule components provide a classification scheme for integrity rules [2].

- **Constraint Type:** Domain/Column/Table (single-row/multi-row)/Database

- **Checking Time:** Immediate/Deferred—For domain, column, or table constraints, such as D1 to D3, C1 to C3, T1 to T3, the DBMS checks for violations immediately. For database constraints, such as DB1—which involve multiple tables and, thus, multiple operations (transactions, or logical units of work)—checking must be deferred to the end of a transaction (referred to as **commit time**), rather than for each of the operations involved [1].

- **Violation Response:** Reject/Compensate—Operations that violate integrity constraints should be rejected by the DBMS. However, in some cases the DBMS can take user-defined compensating actions to neutralize the violation. The best known examples are the referential integrity rules like DB1: Update and delete operations affecting primary key values trigger user mandated cascade actions by the DBMS to adjust referencing foreign key values to avoid inconsistencies (see Chapter 3).

Rule R8, for example, enforcing the no-overlap constraint T3, is a table (single-row), immediate, reject rule. Rules R5, R6, R7, enforcing key constraints T2, T3, T4, respectively, are table (multirow), immediate, reject rules. DB1, enforcing a referential constraint, is a database deferred, reject, and/or compensate rule (see Section 2.3.1).

> ❖ **Note:** Most integrity rules are **state rules**, enforcing constraints on database states: Only the after-update database state is checked for possible violations. Consider now the employee attribute sex, represented by an identically named column. One obvious, if implicit, business rule is "Sex does not change" (well, at least not frequently), which maps to a constraint requiring SEX values not to change. This constraint is not on the after-update state of the database, but rather on the *transition* of the database, via the update, from one state to another; the DBMS must compare the after-state to the before-state to enforce it. Integrity rules enforcing such constraints are **transition rules**.

2.2.5.2 DBMS Support

DBMS integrity support, then, consists of

- Data language facility to declare constraints of all types, of arbitrary complexity

- Inference of constraints on derived tables

- Recording of integrity rules in the database catalog

- Support of all table operations for rule checking

- Deferrable checks

- User-definable violation responses (where appropriate)

If integrity is supported *declaratively*, an intelligent DBMS optimizer can rely on statistics (table length and width, value distributions), index availability, and so on, to group, reorganize, and transform all table operations—including integrity check operations—to maximize performance [7]. (In the no-overlap case, for example, the DBMS can compare *only new* rows to all the other rows in the table, which is more efficient than comparing every row to all other rows.) But if integrity support is *procedural*, via user-written **stored/triggered procedures**, the execution strategy is specified by users in those procedures and, thus, not amenable to optimization by the DBMS, which is much better suited for this task than users. Worse, a procedural execution strategy can interact unpredictably with a nonprocedural update execution and leave the database in an inconsistent state.

2.3 Practical Implications

2.3.1 SQL and Integrity

Except for keys and referential rules, integrity is currently supported only in the advanced level of the SQL standard, the weaknesses and complications of which require dedicated volumes [8]. Only a broad description and assessment of the main features is possible here.

Integrity constraints are declared in SQL as 'CHECK condition' clauses in declarations of integrity statements. SQL does not infer constraints inherited by derived tables (for this reason, it and all its commercial dialects do not permit updating many views that are theoretically updatable, for example, multitable views [4, 5]; in the few cases in which such updates are permitted [e.g., natural join views], the updating algorithms are ad hoc and, thus, cannot always guarantee correctness).

In SQL, domain rules are declared with CREATE DOMAIN statements; column rules are declared as part of CREATE TABLE statements; table and database rules, called ASSERTIONS, are declared with CREATE ASSERTION statements; and table rules can also be declared as part of CREATE TABLE statements. There is no support for transition rules or for direct declaration of functional dependency constraints (see Chapter 8).

Integrity rules can be given user-defined names; otherwise the DBMS will assign them. Checking can be explicitly IMMEDIATE or DEFERRABLE to commit time, but support is partially procedural rather than fully declarative [7]. The violation response is rejection and is implicit for all rules except for CASCADE/SET NULL actions of referential rules (see Chapter 3).

2.3.1.1 Domain Rules

As already explained, a domain (or data type) definition specifies a pool of permissible values and, as such, it is essentially a domain constraint declaration itself. SQL "domains" are not full-fledged data types, but rather "just shared column declarations" with unnecessarily complex support to boot [7] (see Chapter 1).

With these limitations in mind, integrity rules R1, R2, and R3 enforcing the three domain constraints D1, D2, and D3 can be declared in SQL as follows

```
CREATE DOMAIN res# INTEGER(7)
  CONSTRAINT r1
  CHECK (res# > 0 AND res# <= 100000);

CREATE DOMAIN room INTEGER(3)
  CONSTRAINT r2
  CHECK (room => 1 AND room <=350);

CREATE DOMAIN res_date DATE
  CONSTRAINT r3
  CHECK (res_date => '1/10/80');
```

Immediate checking and rejection are implicit in the enforcement of SQL "domain" constraints.

2.3.1.2 Column Rules

As part of CREATE TABLE statements, column rules specify the domain over which columns are defined, or the columns' data types. The rules enforcing the C1, C2, and C3 column constraints are declared as follows

```
CREATE TABLE reserve
  (res# res#,
  room room,
  arr_date res_date,
  dpt_date res_date,
  ...);
```

Immediate checking and rejection are implicit in the enforcement of column constraints.

2.3.1.3 Table and Database Rules

Table and database integrity rules can be declared with CREATE ASSERTION statements. The declaration of rule R4, for example, enforcing the single-row table constraint T1 is declared as follows:

```
CREATE ASSERTION r4
  CHECK (NOT EXISTS
        (SELECT *
         FROM reserve
         WHERE dpt_date < arr_date);
```

Rule R5, enforcing the no-overlap multirow table constraint T5, is declared as follows

```
CREATE ASSERTION r5
  CHECK (NOT EXISTS
        (SELECT *
         FROM reserve r2,reserve r1
         WHERE r2.room = r1.room
           AND r2.res# <> r1.res#
           AND r2.arr_date < r1.dpt_date
           AND r2.dpt_date > r1.arr_date));
```

❖ **Note:** The standard also defines an OVERLAPS operator, which is essentially a shorthand for expressing no-overlap constraints, and, arguably, a somewhat less error-prone formulation, but quirky (see Appendix 2A) due to the complexity induced by SQL's NULLs approach to missing information (see Chapter 10).

Table rules can also be declared as part of CREATE TABLE statements. The following is rule R4, which is embedded in the definition of the RESERVE table. Aside from the column constraints, the RESERVE table also includes the three multirow table rules that enforce the primary and candidate key constraints

```
CREATE TABLE reserve
  (res# res# PRIMARY KEY,
   room room,
   arr_date res_date,
   dpt_date res_date
   UNIQUE (room,arr_date),
   UNIQUE (room,dpt_date),
   CONSTRAINT r5
     CHECK (NOT EXISTS
           (SELECT *
            FROM reserve
            WHERE dpt_date < arr_date));
```

Referential (database) integrity rules, such as DB1, can also be declared as part of CREATE TABLE statements using the foreign key shorthand (see Chapter 3).

```
CREATE TABLE customers
  (cust# cust# PRIMARY KEY,
   name name,
   res# res# FOREIGN KEY
     REFERENCES reserve
     ON UPDATE CASCADE
     ON DELETE CASCADE,
   ...,
   UNIQUE (name));
```

Note the use of CASCADE actions to compensate for potential inconsistency caused by UPDATE and DELETE operations on primary key values.

2.3.2 Procedural Support

The SQL standard does not support CHECK constraints within CREATE TABLE/ASSERTION statements at its entry and intermediate levels (these levels are intended primarily to allow vendors to claim standard compatibility with less than advanced support) and, to date, most commercial DBMSs have not implemented the standard's advanced level integrity features. Some implement integrity procedurally via user-written **stored procedures** expressed in proprietary SQL extensions that can be quite complex, vary across products, and have various limitations (for a potential improvement in portability of procedural languages, see Appendix 1F).

Current DBMS products do not support SQL ASSERTIONs. One widely used product, for example, allows CHECK clauses in CREATE TABLE statements, but the CHECK condition cannot contain subqueries such as the self-join in the no-overlap expression. Consequently, such a constraint must be implemented via the following user-written stored procedure, triggered by table insert and update operations.

```
CREATE TRIGGER r8
ON reserve
FOR INSERT,UPDATE
AS BEGIN
  IF EXISTS
    (SELECT *
     FROM inserted y,reserve x
     WHERE y.room#=x.room#
       AND y.res# <> x.res#
       AND y.dpt_date > x.arr_date
       AND y.arr_date < x.dpt_date)
  ROLLBACK
END
```

The procedure explicitly joins the RESERVE table to a proprietary, internally system-generated temporary table INSERTED (UPDATED for update operations) containing the after-operation rows that are candidates for insertion (or update).

First, this burdens the user with the system's internal way of doing things, such as using temporary tables, specific execution procedures, and commits, which ought to be transparent. Second, by imposing a specific procedure for executing the check operation, the trigger inhibits the DBMS optimizer from selecting more efficient alternatives, should they exist, or from integrating the operation within a global optimization process. Third, such procedures are proprietary and do not work across SQL implementations.

2.4 Conclusion and Recommendations

The sum total of integrity constraints imposed on the database is the best approximation a DBMS has to what the database *means* (the database predicate). The DBMS can, therefore, guarantee correctness if and only if all necessary integrity constraints are declared to and enforceable by it. Any constraint not supported—declaratively or, at the very least, procedurally—must be enforced by users with application code—a burden with extremely costly drawbacks [1], one consequence of which is described at the beginning of this chapter. Indeed, the exact opposite of the first of the three comments initiating this chapter is true: You should enforce integrity with application code *if, not unless* you have a penchant for walking close to the edge.

Whatever the syntax of the data language in which integrity constraints are expressed, an understanding of constraint semantics (meaning) is a necessary prerequisite for both users and the DBMS. There are no substitutes for thorough knowledge of the reality to be represented in the database (of which business rules are an integral part), clear thinking [9], and a logically sound DBMS [1]. Conceptual or logical confusion in the design stage can cause serious difficulties in expressing constraints in any data language, let alone SQL, whose own complexity exacerbates those difficulties (see Chapter 8). "Trying to formulate expressions 'directly' in SQL is too much for the average human brain . . . One of my criticisms of all levels of SQL prior to SQL92 was precisely that it was not as powerful as the [relational] calculus—that is not 'relationally complete'—and you could not tell whether or not [it could solve] a given problem" [10].

❖ **Note:** Consider, for example, the difficulty a user had expressing the no-overlap constraint in SQL:

> *At first, I thought that the OVERLAPS condition (in SQL) could somehow be used. Unfortunately, I quickly discovered that my DBMS does not support [it]. I then thought about using the BETWEEN operator in conjunction with COUNT() [in a CREATE TABLE CHECK clause]:*

```
CHECK ((SELECT COUNT(arr_date)
          FROM reserve
          WHERE arr_date BETWEEN arr_date AND dpt_date)=1);
```

> *This, however, causes a recursive operation that completely discombobulates my database server. It is also incomplete—it does not prevent [rows] that completely enclose other's rows' time intervals, nor rows [with intervals] that begin before that of other rows, but end smack in the middle of [other] rows. Tricky!*

The attempted expression is incorrect, of course, because just like (1 BETWEEN 1 AND 2), it *always* evaluates to either 'true' or to 'false' depending on whether BETWEEN means < and > or <= and >=.

The implications for integrity can be particularly insidious because such complications can lead to the formulation of *syntactically valid, yet semantically wrong* constraints and, thus, to data corruption of which *there is no awareness* (see Chapter 5 for an example).

The data language should permit users to express—and the DBMS should enforce—wherever possible, integrity constraints of arbitrary complexity declaratively rather than procedurally. Stored procedures—whether triggered or not—are preferable to application level integrity code, but they are practically inferior to and riskier than declarative support [3] because they are more burdensome to write, error prone, and cannot benefit from full DBMS optimization.

Users are well advised to

- Design fully normalized databases in order to minimize the number of constraints to be declared, checked, and enforced (see Chapter 5).

- Familiarize themselves with logic and the four constraint categories: domain, column, table, and database.

- Choose DBMSs with better declarative integrity support. Given the considerable gaps in such support by products, knowledgeable users would be at least in a position to emulate *correctly*—albeit with procedural and/or application code—constraints not supported by the DBMS.

- Modularize and document all procedural and application constraints.

- Be on constant alert and check databases frequently for undetected integrity violations.

Aside from reducing the risk of invalid data, this approach will sensitize users to the burdens imposed by product deficiencies and lead them to demand the only true solution: full and correct integrity support from DBMS vendors.

References

[1] F. Pascal, *Understanding Relational Databases*, New York, NY: John Wiley & Sons, 1993.

[2] C. J. Date, "Integrity Revisited," *Relational Database Writings 1994–1997*, Reading, MA: Addison-Wesley, 1998.

[3] C. J. Date and D. McGoveran, "A New Database Design Principle," *Relational Database Writings 1991–1994*, Reading, MA: Addison-Wesley, 1995.

[4] C. J. Date and D. McGoveran, "Updating Union, Intersection and Difference Views," *Relational Database Writings 1991–1994*, Reading, MA: Addison-Wesley, 1995.

[5] C. J. Date and D. McGoveran, "Updating Joins and Other Views," *Relational Database Writings 1991–1994*, Reading, MA: Addison-Wesley, 1995.

[6] C. J. Date and H. Darwen, *The Third Manifesto, Foundation for Object/Relational Databases*, Reading, MA: Addison-Wesley, 1998.

[7] C. J. Date, "A Matter of Integrity," *Relational Database Writings 1991–1994*, Parts 1–3, Reading, MA: Addison-Wesley, 1995.

[8] C. J. Date and H. Darwen, *Guide to the SQL Standard,* 4th ed., Reading, MA: Addison-Wesley, 1997.

[9] C. J. Date, "Why It Is Important to Think Precisely," *Relational Database Writings 1994–1997*, Parts 1–4, Reading, MA: Addison-Wesley, 1998.

[10] C. J. Date, personal communication, 1999.

A Note on SQL's OVERLAPS Operator

The SQL standard defines an OVERLAPS operator for testing whether the intervals between two pairs of dates or times overlap [1]. Like BETWEEN, it is a comparison operator taking the form

```
row-constructor OVERLAPS row-constructor
```

where 'row-constructor' contains values of type date/time. It is simply a shorthand for expressing overlap (or no-overlap) conditions. Given a row with the reservation (9/12/96,10/25/96), for example, the overlap condition for any other row (ARR_DATE,DPT_DATE)

```
arr_date < DATE '1996-10-25' AND dpt_date > DATE '1996-9-12'
```

can be expressed in standard SQL as

```
(arr_date,dpt_date) OVERLAPS (DATE '1996-9-12',DATE '1996-10-25')
```

which evaluates to true for rows that overlap and false for rows that do not. The constraint for the RESERVE table in the chapter would be

```
CHECK
  (NOT EXISTS
     (SELECT *
      FROM reserve y,reserve x
      WHERE y.room# = x.room#
        AND (y.arr_date,y.dpt_date)
      OVERLAPS (x.arr_date,x.dpt_date)));
```

Whether OVERLAPS is "better" is in the eye of the beholder, although it is probably somewhat less prone to error than using BETWEEN and ANDs, particularly if the direct expression must take NULLs into account. Consider the reservations

R1:   (9/20/96,9/25/96)

R2:   (9/25/96,9/31/96)

R3:   (9/25/96,9/25/96) <-- zero length interval!

where D1 coincides with both A2 and (A3, D3). An OVERLAPS expression yields no overlap for R1 and overlap for R2. This "ugly asymmetry" occurs because standard SQL needs to "bend over backwards" to avoid the problems that NULLs cause for comparisons [2]. It defines

```
(Ay,Dy) OVERLAPS (Ax,Dx)
```

not as

```
Ay < Dx AND Dy > Ax
```

but rather as

```
(Ay > Ax AND (Ay < Dx OR Dy < Dx)) OR
(Ax > Ay AND (Ax < Dy OR Dx < Dy)) OR
(ay = Ax AND Ay IS NOT NULL AND Ax IS NOT NULL)
```

Now, zero-length *lodging* reservations are not likely. Nevertheless, they may occur in different overlap contexts and, besides, data languages should not suffer from quirks with odd consequences. This is yet another example of how SQL NULLs cause problems and complicate the language (see Chapter 10).

Commercial SQL DBMSs do not currently support the OVERLAPS shorthand.

References

[1] C. J. Date and Hugh Darwen, *Guide to the SQL Standard*, 4th ed., Reading, MA: Addison-Wesley, 1997.

[2] C. J. Date, personal communication, 1999.

3

A Matter of Identity: Keys

Do I have to add a column [with unique values] to be able to access a particular row? Or is there something that exists which I can use?
—ONLINE MESSAGE

I know exactly what relational means. I just objected to you saying that a table must have a primary key. "Must" to me means that a table cannot physically be added to, or exist in a database if it doesn't have a PK. [T]hat's absurd. That it should have a PK in most cases is unarguable. But certainly a table can be created without any key or index. Perhaps in some cases I can't imagine it really makes sense to do so.
—ONLINE MESSAGE

I'm having difficulty creating a table with one of the columns in a composite primary key being NULL[able]. Example: table ABC with columns in the PK 'A' NOT NULL, 'B' NOT NULL, and 'C' NULL. Logically, I have a valid business reason for wanting to implement a table with at least one column of the compound PK being nullable.
—ONLINE MESSAGE

Our database was designed almost exclusively with tables utilizing surrogate keys—specifically self-incrementing integer values—as primary keys . . . This may be a mistake because of the added complexity with our foreign keys when using report-writers against our databases . . . [and] the added time involved in making the necessary joins . . . for instance, in the EMPLOYEES table, columns SKILL_LEVEL, SCODE, and P_S_LEVEL [are foreign keys] containing integer values pointing to their respective primary key values . . . the user or the report writer will need to make joins to make each employee record understandable.
—ONLINE MESSAGE

3.1 The Issue

Whether keys are necessary and, if so, how to choose them are two of the most commonly raised questions about databases. This is yet another example of the poor understanding of, and confusion about the most fundamental issues in database management in general and relational technology in particular. SQL and its commercial implementations, which initially lacked key support altogether and now make keys optional, are not the only contributors to this state of affairs. The object approach has made its own contribution by advocating object IDs, which are a throwback to pointers, but which many practitioners confuse with surrogate keys.

This chapter

- Defines and explains the key concept

- Discusses the various types of keys

- Provides criteria for the choice of keys

- Clarifies what proper DBMS support of keys means

- Demonstrates some practical implications of weak key support in SQL

3.2 Fundamentals

Entities are uniquely identifiable in the real world, or we would not be able to tell them apart. Indeed, we cannot refer to a specific entity—say, an employee—except by some distinguishing attribute. That is why we give persons names, cars license plates, and so on: These become "natural" identifiers, attributes guaranteeing uniqueness such that we can refer to each and every entity without ambiguity. When there is no natural identifier as with, say, cereal boxes, and we need to refer to *individual* boxes, we distinguish between them either visually—by pointing to their physical location in space ("this one, that one")—or by assigning them some arbitrary identifier "on the fly," so to speak ("one, two, three").

Databases represent assertions of fact—propositions—about entities of interest in the real world. The representation must be correct—only true propositions (facts) must be represented. Therefore, the attribute(s) identifying entities must be represented in the database and *known to the DBMS;* otherwise it, as well as users, will not be able to refer to (address) individual rows or even know how many distinct entities are there (see Chapter 4). Identifying attributes are represented in the database by **key columns**, whose values must obviously be unique. Note in particular that if key values are missing, the DBMS cannot guarantee uniqueness and row identification will be defeated. Consequently, key values cannot be allowed to be missing (missing information is discussed in detail in Chapter 10).

Keys are a shorthand for a type of integrity constraint—specifically, a table constraint (see Chapter 2)—that represents in the database a **functional dependency** between entity attributes in the real world; every nonkey column in a fully normalized table is functionally dependent on the key column(s) (see Chapter 5). For example, in the EMPLOYEES table in Figure 3.1, where EMP# is key, DEPT#, HIRE-DATE, and SALARY are functionally dependent on EMP# as follows:

```
EMP# → DEPT#
EMP# → HIREDATE
EMP# → SALARY
```

EMP#	ENAME	DEPT#	HIREDATE	SALARY
20	Thompson	B01	10-10-1973	41250
30	Kwan	C01	04-05-1975	40175
50	Geyer	E01	08-17-1949	38250
60	Stern	D11	09-14-1973	36250

Figure 3.1. *Functional Dependencies*

Together with value "atomicity" and proper table and column naming (see Chapters 1 and 5), keys provide a simple addressing scheme that guarantees *logical* access to each and every value in the database: 'table name + column name + key value'. In the absence of keys or *DBMS knowledge of them*, duplicate rows can occur in the database, resulting in loss of integrity and other deleterious effects (see Chapter 4)—for example, the addressing scheme breaks down and view updatability is defeated.

The **criterion for update acceptability** for a table is the **table's predicate**, the generalized form of the **propositions** represented by the table's rows [6]. To guarantee correctness, any update operation on the table that violates its predicate (that is, results in rows that represent propositions that are not true) should be rejected by the DBMS. The best approximation of a table predicate on which the DBMS can base its update decisions is the sum total of integrity constraints on the table, which include **key constraints** (uniqueness). Database correctness is predicated, therefore, on DBMS enforcement of all table constraints, including key constraints (see Chapter 2).

Views are derived tables, and, as such, they inherit their predicates from the base tables over which they are defined. Courtesy of relational theory, key constraints for a derived table, together with all other constraints [7], can be inferred logically from the base tables' constraints and the table operations used for the derivation. When, for example, a join is applied to tables A and B to produce a join table C, if the RDBMS knows the constraints on the two input tables A and B, it can infer the constraints on the output view C and, thus, it can decide whether any update of C violates those constraints or not. **Key inheritance**—inferring the keys of views [8]—is crucial for a DBMS's ability to propagate view updates to the underlying base tables correctly (see Chapter 2). Full DBMS key support is necessary (though not sufficient) to guarantee logical access, view updatability, and database correctness.

> ❖ **Note:** Formally, keyless tables do not have the properties of mathematical sets, are not relational tables, and a database containing them cannot benefit practically from the theoretical foundations of the relational model.

3.2.1 Simple versus Composite Keys

When entities in the real world are identified by one attribute, the attribute is represented in the database by a one-column **simple key**. But there are circumstances where identification requires a combination of attributes. The most common example is names. There can well be, for example, more than one employee with the same last name, so a combination of the last and first names may be necessary to guarantee uniqueness. Another example is associative entities, such as shipments, which can be viewed as associations of a product (identified by product number) with a customer (identified by customer number) and, thus, are identified by product and customer number combinations. Multiattribute identifiers are represented in the database by multicolumn **composite keys** [1].

Composite keys must have the property of **irreducibility**: Uniqueness must apply to the *whole* key, not just to a component column or subcombinations thereof. Thus, if the last name alone is *always unique*, then the first and last name column combination is not irreducible. The {EMP#,DEPT#} combination is irreducible if employee numbers are not unique across the company.

> ❖ **Note:** Keys are a *logical* feature and should not be confused, as they often are, with **indexes**, which are a *physical* feature to improve performance. Some of the confusion is due to SQL DBMSs implementing keys via unique indexes in a way that violates data independence (see Section 3.3.1).

3.2.2 Natural versus Surrogate Keys

In a sense, no identifier in the real world is natural. Indeed, we *assign* names, social security numbers, policy numbers, employee numbers, car licenses, and so on precisely because there aren't any inherent ones. However, once assigned and used in the real world, these identifiers become natural and the columns representing them in the database are **natural keys**. For database purposes, then, a key is deemed natural if the attribute it represents was used for identification prior to (and, thus, independently of) the database. Natural keys have the advantage of **familiarity**—they are meaningful to users.

But when natural identifiers do not precede the database, as in the cereal box case, and individual entities are of interest, the visual/ arbitrary on the fly identifiers can be represented in the database by columns with, say, sequential integer values. Such columns are **surrogate keys**: They do not identify entities in a *meaningful* manner, like natural keys, they just *distinguish* between them in arbitrary fashion. Note that by this definition, columns, such as EMP#, can be natural keys (if employee numbers precede the database), or surrogate keys (if they were created expressly for the database).

There are many instances where surrogate keys are useful even if natural keys exist. As mentioned previously, employee names yield a composite natural key consisting of at least two columns, {LNAME,FNAME}. Composite keys can be cumbersome (and prone to error) in use. Moreover, names can change, and **stability** is a desirable property for identifiers. Familiarity notwithstanding, names would not yield a "good" key on **simplicity** grounds either (see next Note), which is precisely why surrogate keys, such as EMP#, ACCT#, CUST#, and so on are issued even when a natural identifier exists.

> ❖ **Note:** Identical last and first names are also possible, in which case a
> third key column would be required, say, middle initial; but it may not
> guarantee uniqueness either, and, besides, not everybody has a middle
> name. Nonnumeric keys may have performance implications, but this is a
> *physical implementation* issue, completely separate from *logical* consider-
> ations on the basis of which key choices should be made.

3.2.3 Candidate versus Primary Keys

Codd's original formulation of the relational model requires every table
to have a **primary key**. When entities of a type have one identifying
attribute, there is only one key, so primacy is moot. The primacy issue
arises only when there is more than one identifying attribute and,
hence, multiple **candidate keys**. In such cases, one of the candidate
keys would have to be selected as primary key. But what is the purpose of this requirement, and on what grounds should the choice be
made?

As already mentioned, long nonnumeric, composite, or volatile columns make cumbersome keys. Consider, for example, the real-world
database of a health-care provider, where the organization deemed the
simplicity and stability of a surrogate key more useful relative to the
composite and possibly volatile {LNAME,FNAME} natural key and
assigned patients a 12-digit identifier, NBUNIT, such that the
PATIENTS table had two candidate keys, one simple and one
composite.

```
PATIENTS {NBUNIT,LNAME,FNAME,...}
```

Whether one is chosen as primary key or not, users can, depending on
preferences, rely on either of the keys for logical access. The DBMS

can enforce uniqueness for both keys and use the surrogate key for performance optimization purposes even if user access to the database is by name. Indeed, forcing the choice of a primary key seems to reduce flexibility, and recently an argument for the relaxation of the mandatory primary key requirement was advanced:

> In all . . . [formal] research it is candidate keys, not primary keys, that play the crucial role. Given that this is so, it really does not seem appropriate to insist formally on the primacy of primary keys—[al]though it may be appropriate to recommend it informally . . . while the [mandatory primary key] rules in question can be seen as good guidelines that should certainly be followed in the majority of practical situations, they are indeed only guidelines, and sometimes there are good reasons for violating them. [2]

Otherwise put, choosing one key as primary, although a good idea in most cases, should not be obligatory in all circumstances. But why is the choice—albeit, informal—of a primary key a good idea in *any* circumstance?

3.2.4 Foreign Keys

In view of the principle that *all* information in a relational database should be uniformly represented as rows of column values in tables—Codd's fundamental **information rule**—so must be logical relationships be between rows across tables; **foreign keys** are the mechanism for representing them. A foreign key is a column (or combination of columns) in one table whose values reference key values in another table [3].

In the health-care database, for example, every row in the ADMISSIONS table referenced some row in the PATIENTS table, but some patients had more than one hospital admission. This many-to-one relationship between admissions and patients was represented by a foreign key column in the ADMISSIONS table, whose values reference key values in the PATIENTS table (any admission row for a patient not recorded in PATIENTS would put the database in an inconsistent state by violating the business rule "admission information exists only for patients of record"). The DBMS had to enforce a **referential constraint**, a type of database integrity constraint, to prevent such inconsistencies (see Chapter 2). But the PATIENTS table had two candidate keys, so which should ADMISSIONS reference?

> ❖ **Note:** Obviously, the referencing foreign key values and referenced key values must be of the same data type (in relational terms, drawn from the same domain). This is another way of saying that the values must be *meaningfully comparable* [3]; that is, the two columns represent the same attribute (see Chapter 1).

3.2.4.1 Referential Integrity and Primary Keys

Without a *formal* criterion for preferring one candidate key over the other, foreign keys could reference *either, or both*. For example, ADMISSIONS could reference NBUNIT and another table could reference {LNAME,FNAME}. "Multikey" referential integrity complicates DBMS implementation for vendors and database access for users. The complications are exacerbated by composite keys [4]. Choosing one of the keys as primary, especially a simple rather than a composite one, and referencing it alone, simplifies matters considerably.

Thus, the mandatory primary key requirement is, essentially, a *pragmatic* one: simplification of referential integrity. However, unlike **normalization rules**, which, being based on **dependency theory**, are formal and apply generally to all databases (see Chapter 5), the pragmatic criteria for primary key selection—familiarity, simplicity, and stability—are not formal and, as recognized by the founder of relational technology, outside the scope of the (formal) **data model**. Choosing between candidates, such as NBUNIT and {LNAME,FNAME}, means trading these criteria off (here, familiarity for simplicity and stability). The optimal trade-off point is subjective and can vary across databases, users, and even time.

> ❖ **Note:** A common attempt to eschew such trade-offs is to "overload" key columns, that is, to encode several facts into them. In the health-care provider case, for example, the 12 digits of NBUNIT were a concatenation of several codes that were meaningful within the organization (e.g., 324 44 56-1 9400). Such **"intelligent" keys**, as they are often called, create the impression that *both* the complexity of composite natural keys and the lack of familiarity of surrogate keys can be avoided. However, "intelligent" is actually a misnomer because this is hardly an intelligent key choice. It is just the opposite: It does not avoid the trade-offs, but rather obscures the need to make them. Encoding more than one fact (attribute) in a column violates first normal form (see Chapter 5) because information is represented *implicitly* in the internal composition of the values—rather than explicitly as separate values, as relationally required—and, as such, it is inaccessible to the DBMS. It makes things worse: If *any* of the components change, *all* applications accessing the key column will be affected, defeating stability. Either the information encoded in the key is meaningful, in which case it should be represented *explicitly* and made accessible to the DBMS for integrity enforcement and manipulation purposes; or it is not, in which case why record it at all? It makes no sense to record meaningful information but "hide" it from the DBMS.

Relaxing the primary key requirement from mandatory to "desirable in most cases" should not be taken, therefore, as license for casually allowing tables with only candidate keys in the database. The relaxation is intended only to distinguish the pragmatic primary key requirement from the other formal, theory-based relational requirements.

In fact, closer inspection of circumstances in which the choice of a primary key is deemed "entirely arbitrary" reveals that this is not exactly so [2]. Consider the table

`EXAMS {STUDENT,SUBJECT,RANK}`

An exam is an association of a student with a subject that has as an attribute the student's class ranking on that subject. Every exam is uniquely identified by either the {STUDENT,SUBJECT} or the {SUBJECT,RANK} combination. It's argued that there is no good reason to prefer one over the other as primary key. And indeed, *if EXAMS were not referenced by any other table*, there would be no reason to choose. But a simple primary key would be preferable to a composite key for referential purposes, so a surrogate key, say, EXAM#, should probably be defined and chosen as primary key, which would obviate the need to choose between the two composite natural keys. (Note also that if potential RANK ties are taken into account, there is actually *only one three-column natural key*, which makes the case for a simple surrogate primary key even more compelling.)

Similar arguments apply to the table

`ROSTERS {DAY,HOUR,GATE,PILOT}`

where {DAY,HOUR,PILOT} and {DAY,HOUR,GATE} are candidate keys. A surrogate key would be useful, which is precisely why flight numbers are used by the airline industry

`ROSTERS {FLIGHT#,DAY,HOUR,GATE,PILOT}`

with {FLIGHT#,DAY} as the most likely candidate for primary key (of course, a ROSTER# simple surrogate key could also be defined and selected as primary key for referential purposes).

The tables

```
INVOICES {INV#,SHIP#,...}
SHIPMENTS {SHIP#,INV#,...}
```

represent a one-to-one relationship between shipments and invoices. But here the primary key choice dilemma is caused by the inclusion of both identifiers in both tables. Neither table represents an associative entity type, so this redundancy is unnecessary for identification purposes. The problem could be avoided by using either of the following two designs

```
INVOICES {INV#,...}
SHIPMENTS {SHIP#,INV#,...}

INVOICES {INV#,SHIP#,...}
SHIPMENTS {SHIP#,...}
```

which, incidentally, would be preferable on familiarity grounds: If invoices and shipments are entities of distinct types—the reason for using two tables in the first place—it makes sense to identify invoices by INV# and shipments by SHIP#. The one-table design option would actually make a much better case for the relaxation argument

```
INV_SHIP {SHIP#,INV#,...}
```

There is, of course, nothing to prohibit tables with only candidate keys (which *are*, of course, mandatory). The point is, though, that such an approach is not free of drawbacks, and *in referential contexts*, the drawbacks arising from the absence of a primary key tend to override those arising from (albeit informal) primary key selections.

3.2.5 DBMS Support

DBMS key support consists of the following:

- Enforcement of key constraints (candidate and primary)

- Enforcement of at least one mandatory key for each table, simple or composite

- Rejection of missing (including partially missing) key values

- Enforcement of foreign keys and referential constraints for update, insert, and delete operations with restrict and cascade options [3]

- Inference of key inheritance by derived tables

A DBMS **key generation facility** is also recommended [4]. The data language would "provide a mechanism according to which values of some key (or certain components thereof) for some specified table are supplied by the system. It should also provide a mechanism according to which an arbitrary table can be extended to include an attribute whose values are *(a)* unique within that table (or within certain partitions of that table) and *(b)* are once again supplied by the system" [5]. For example, consider a research database to be derived from the health-care database for statistical analysis purposes. Aggregate analysis does not require meaningful identification of rows, only the ability to distinguish between them. Neither the simple, but long surrogate key NBUNIT, nor the composite key {LNAME,FNAME} would be very practical for referential purposes (and would raise confidentiality issues to boot). A simple numeric surrogate key, say, PAT#, with sequentially ascending values, could be used, and it would be practical for the DBMS, rather than a user-written application to generate PAT# values. More sophisticated system key generation would particularly benefit databases representing hierarchies, such as organizational or assembly tree structures (see Chapter 7).

> ❖ **Note:** Some practitioners influenced by the object approach recommend system-assigned surrogate keys for all tables. Although nothing precludes this approach, there is no convincing justification for universal deployment of system-generated surrogate keys. Thorough knowledge of the reality to be represented in the database and of how the database will be used should inform a more selective use of such keys, based on the aforementioned criteria.

The practical importance of full and correct key support is demonstrated by the consequences of deficient support by SQL and its commercial implementations.

3.3 Practical Implications

3.3.1 SQL and Keys

The initial version of the SQL standard did not support keys. A subsequent addendum added limited support for keys and referential integrity, which was implemented to various degrees by commercial DBMSs. But having been added post hoc, the implementations are riddled with numerous restrictions and exceptions, which rendered them quite complex. Furthermore, keys are to this day still *optional* in SQL. In part, this was to avoid invalidating existing keyless databases for already written applications, but it was also due to the unfortunate opinion of the ANSI SQL standard committee—the committee's own use of *unique identifiers* for tracking its research papers notwithstanding—that keys need not be mandatory. Indeed, the committee deems duplicates to be desirable at times. So much so that the relational UNION operation, which correctly eliminates duplicates from the result, has been modified in SQL to optionally *preserve* them in the result. (The UNION ALL nonrelational version of the operation is used for recursive operations on tree-structured databases, with deleterious effects for users, see Chapter 7.)

It is in large part because of this history that, as the examples at the start of this chapter indicate, many practitioners think that keys are not always necessary and that leaving them optional "adds flexibility." Optional keys are, of course, a case of *spurious* flexibility. One consequence in practice is a high frequency of duplicate rows, allowed either inadvertently or even intentionally in databases, with quite serious repercussions (see Chapter 4). Saddled with the burden of locating, interpreting, and deleting duplicates (see Appendix 4A), users blame

SQL for not facilitating duplicate elimination, instead of correctly blaming it for failure to mandate keys that would have prevented the duplicates from entering the database in the first place (see Chapter 4).

Limited view updatability in SQL is also due to deficient key support. As already explained, integrity constraints on views—including key constraints—can be logically inferred from the constraints and keys of the input tables and the operations used to derive the views, but *only if the tables and the operations are relational.* And relational tables are, by definition, in first normal form (or normalized), which means they have keys [3] (see Chapter 5). Under these conditions, many multitable views are updatable [6, 9]. But if nonrelational keyless tables are allowed, constraint inferences including key inheritance, cannot be made. Lacking the update acceptability criterion for views, the DBMS is unable to guarantee the correct propagation of view updates to the underlying base tables.

This explains why SQL DBMSs do not permit updates on multitable views, views defined with DISTINCT, and so on, even though they are theoretically updatable. This seriously impairs **logical data independence**, a significant practical benefit of relational technology [3]. Because keys were not an integral part of SQL initially and because they were added later as only an option, SQL-based DBMSs could not count on them, so to avoid database corruption, they simply prohibit multitable view updates altogether. Note very carefully that for this reason, multitable views are not updatable *even when keys are defined by users* for all tables, which demonstrates that there is more to key support than just key definition and uniqueness enforcement facilities.

SQL DBMSs typically enforce key constraints by uniquely indexing key columns. But although SQL insulates users and applications from indexes by not requiring explicit reference to them in data manipulation (the DBMS optimizer uses them transparently wherever appropriate), SQL DBMSs still violate physical data independence by

DEPT#	DEPTNAME	MGR#
B01	Planning	20
C01	Information Center	30
E01	Support Services	50
D11	Manufacturing Systems	60
D21	Administration Systems	70
E11	Operations	90
E21	Software Support	100

Figure 3.2. *DEPARTMENTS Table*

making a *logical* integrity constraint—uniqueness—dependent on a *physical* implementation detail—a specific access method—that should be used only if and when it enhances performance. Consequently, indexes on key columns cannot be dropped or replaced with other access methods to suit different performance requirements (a *reduction* in flexibility). This is not to say that key columns should not be indexed; instead indexes are recommended because keys are frequently used for searches. The point is, rather, that physical details should be modifiable at will without affecting the logical level, which is not possible for SQL key indexes.

There are all sorts of other quirks in SQL that could be avoided with correct and full support of keys, the knowledge of which could be exploited by the DBMS for the users' benefit [10]. For example, suppose that in addition to the EMPLOYEES table in Figure 3.1, there is a DEPARTMENTS table, shown in Figure 3.2.

The query

```
SELECT d.dept#,d.mgr#,AVG(e.salary)
FROM departments d,employees e
WHERE d.dept#=e.dept#
GROUP BY d.dept#
```

is invalid in standard SQL because "MGR is neither an aggregate function, nor a column specified in the GROUP BY clause [and thus] is disallowed in the SELECT-list" [10]. The SQL requirement to have MGR# in the GROUP BY list (even if there is no interest in it) is not intuitive, and the user may not understand why the query fails without it. But as a nonkey column, DNAME is *functionally dependent* on the key DEPT# (see Chapter 5), and "if the system were able to recognize this dependency, it could allow MGR# to be omitted from the GROUP BY clause even if it is specified in the SELECT-list. And the query would probably then run a little faster, thanks to the reduction in the number of grouping columns" [10].

Another example of how knowledge of keys could be exploited to optimize performance is the query

```
SELECT DISTINCT e.emp#,e.ename,d.mgr
FROM employees e,departments d
WHERE e.dept# = d.dept#
```

Because EMP# is a key and the operation is a primary key–foreign key join, the DBMS could infer that result rows will be distinct and, therefore, could execute the query the same way regardless of whether DISTINCT is used or not. But because SQL DBMSs do not make such inferences, DISTINCT slows down performance. "Furthermore, a view defined . . . with DISTINCT should be just as updatable as that [without it], even though SQL says it is not" [10].

3.4 Conclusion and Recommendations

Keys are an integral part of accurate database representation of the real world. They enable a simple addressing scheme that guarantees logical access to each and every database value. By preventing duplicates, they ensure database correctness and preserve the set properties of tables from which many practical benefits derive; among them, view updatability and logical data independence, better usability, and faster performance.

Even if the DBMS does not provide full and correct support of keys, users should not take *dis*advantage of key optionality in SQL and should define at least one for every table and a primary key for tables with multiple keys that are referenced by other tables. Users should also expect, demand, and prefer DBMSs with an intelligent key generation facility.

References

[1] C. J. Date, "Integrity Revisited," *Relational Database Writings 1994–1997*, Reading, MA: Addison-Wesley, 1998.

[2] C. J. Date, "The Primacy of Primary Keys: An Investigation," *Relational Database Writings 1991–1994*, Reading, MA: Addison-Wesley, 1995.

[3] F. Pascal, *Understanding Relational Databases*, New York, NY: John Wiley & Sons, 1993.

[4] H. Darwen, "The Duplicity of Duplicate Rows," *Relational Database Writings 1989–1991*, Reading, MA: Addison-Wesley, 1992.

[5] C. J. Date, "Composite Keys" and "Composite Foreign Keys and Nulls," *Relational Database Writings 1989–1991*, Reading, MA: Addison-Wesley, 1992.

[6] C. J. Date, "Updating Union, Intersection and Difference Views," *Relational Database Writings 1991–1994*, Reading, MA: Addison-Wesley, 1995.

[7] C. J. Date, "Relations and Their Meaning," *Database Programming and Design*, December 1994.

[8]   H. Darwen, "The Keys of the Kingdom," *Relational Database Writings 1985–1989*, Reading, MA: Addison-Wesley, 1990.

[9]   C. J. Date, "Updating Joins and Other Views," *Relational Database Writings 1991–1994*, Reading, MA: Addison-Wesley, 1995.

[10]   C. J. Date, "The Role of Functional Dependence in Query Decomposition," *Relational Database Writings 1991–1994*, Reading, MA: Addison-Wesley, 1995.

4

Don't Get Duped
by Dupes: Duplicate Rows

*Ever been to a supermarket? Maybe you can see the difference among
30 boxes of cake mix, all with the same manufacturing lot number, but
most people won't care. Ever voted on something, where everyone writes
their choice on a piece of paper and puts it in a box? Certainly the
ballots are not identical, even when they specify the same candidate,
but in tabulating the votes, that is not supposed to matter.*

—ONLINE COMMENT

*In a table I copied to Sybase, I discovered there was a duplicate row.
What is the best way to eliminate it? I ended up just truncating the table
and recopying, but I am wondering if there is a clean way to eliminate a
duplicate row that already exists?*

—ONLINE COMMENT

*There are two ways to delete duplicate data in Oracle: Write an Oracle
Pro*C program with embedded SQL DELETE statements . . . or use
a . . . correlated subquery . . . or a DELETE statement relying on
ROWIDs] . . . [such statements have] to perform full table scans and a
set of complex operations . . . [which] will be very slow. Using an Oracle
ROWID is also dangerous because it is an Oracle proprietary [physical]
column that could change between Oracle product releases.*
*SQL . . . operates on sets of data . . . This makes life simple for the SQL
DBMS user, at least most of the time. There are some cases where the
lack of a procedural language can impact your ability to manage your
data. For example, eliminating duplicate data table rows.*

—USER GROUP NEWSLETTER

4.1 The Issue

Many in the database field (including the ANSI SQL committee) insist that there is no compelling reason for mandatory keys. Yet the tolerance of duplicates by SQL and its commercial implementations leads the very same practitioners to complain of difficulties in deleting duplicate rows from SQL databases. The inconsistency escapes them. Duplicates have a plethora of deleterious effects, but conceptual confusion and a poor understanding of what database representation means prevent users from being aware of and associating those problems with their real cause. Neither are most users aware that a second kind of duplicate rows—those *across* tables—have equally problematic implications for database practice.

This chapter

- Explains what duplicate rows mean

- Demonstrates their consequences for database practice

- Offers practical recommendations

4.2 Fundamentals

Consider the table in Figure 4.1, representing cake mix boxes. Purportedly, the duplicate rows reflect the fact that boxes are identical.

Description	Price
Cake mix	1.10
Cake mix	1.10

Figure 4.1. *Representation with Duplicates*

But database rows represent propositions of fact asserted to be true. The duplicates in Figure 4.1 represent, therefore, the following propositions

> *Item named* **Cake mix box** *has price $1.10*

> *Item named* **Cake mix box** *has price $1.10*

or, in other words, the same proposition stated twice. Asserting something more than once does not make it more true [1], only redundant. Yet many claim that recording the same proposition more than once has informational value: The number of rows (here, two), they argue, tells us how many entities (here, boxes) there are in the real world.

But, in fact, duplicate rows can *prevent* users from knowing the actual number of boxes in the real world.

4.2.1 Determining Entity Types

At issue is the informational intent of the database: What types of entities do database tables represent? With respect to the table in Figure 4.1, are the attributes of interest about the cake mix box *in general*, or about *individual* boxes? The propositions should be formulated accordingly. If the interest is in individual boxes, propositions should include the identity fact—that attribute which distinguishes each box from the others.

What is the distinguishing attribute of otherwise identical entities, such as cake mix boxes? In the real world, we distinguish between such entities visually by their distinct locations in physical space. Without such distinction it would be logically impossible to even know that there are multiple entities. Indeed, *entities are countable only if they are distinguishable.* Considering that in the real world all entities *are* distinguishable, duplicates represent indistinguishable entities and, therefore, are an inaccurate representation of reality. In a correct representation, propositions about individual boxes would, therefore, have to include a box identifier, say, a box number, which is the equivalent to the visual "this" versus "that" distinction in the real world.

Box **1** *named* **Cake mix** *has price* $1.10

Box **2** *named* **Cake mix** *has price* $1.10

The identifier is represented in the database by a surrogate key (see Chapter 3), shown in Figure 4.2A. If, on the other hand, the entity type of interest is the box in general, it should be represented as one row, as seen in Figure 4.2B, with the count made explicit. Note that in both cases the tables have keys and, therefore, neither representation involves duplicates.

4.2.2 "Hidden" Information

Consider the table in Figure 4.3, recording birds in order of arrival at a feeding location [2]. The rows represent propositions that do not contain the arrival order attribute, which is implicit ("hidden") in the row order. Consequently, unlike the boxes table in Figure 4.1, the birds table would lose that information if reordered.

This can be avoided by representing arrival order explicitly without duplicates. The principle is the same as in the box case: representing the distinguishing attribute (here, arrival order) by a column, as seen in Figure 4.4. Except that here the distinction is not arbitrary, like the box number, but carries *meaning*. Note that this version of the table can be reordered without loss of information.

Box	Description	Price
1	Cake mix	1.10
2	Cake mix	1.10

A. Individual boxes as entities

Descripton	Price	Quantity
Cake mix	1.10	2

B. Box category as entity

Figure 4.2. *Representations of Different Propositions*

Bird
Sparrow
Blue Tit
Great Tit
Robin
Blue Tit
Blue Tit

Bird	Arrival
Robin	4
Blue Tit	6
Sparrow	1
Blue Tit	2
Great Tit	3
Blue Tit	5

Figure 4.3. *Duplicates with Essential Ordering*

Figure 4.4. *Order Made Explicit*

❖ **Note:** The table in Figure 4.1 also represents information implicitly—the row count. In that case, the implicit information is not lost via reshuffling; it is rather unreliable (see Section 4.3.1.2). The information in the birds table can also be represented without duplicates in a way similar to that in Figure 4.2A, but with *loss of information.*

Bird	Count
Robin	1
Sparrow	1
Great Tit	1
Blue Tit	3

4.2.3 A Relational Bonus

Avoiding duplicates is, first and foremost, a matter of representation accuracy—any database, regardless of underlying technology, must represent the real world of interest completely and correctly.

1. Entities are distinguishable (uniquely identifiable) in the real world;

2. Therefore, entity representatives [records] must be distinguishable in the database [3];

For tables without duplicates the relational model simply adds a major advantage—a dual theoretical foundation. One component is **set theory**.

3. So we need a theory of unique objects that can be adapted to our database purpose;

4. Set [relational] theory is such a theory [3].

The other is **predicate logic**. "A database is a set of **axioms**. The response to a query is a **theorem**. The process of deriving the theorem from the axioms is a **proof**. The proof is made by manipulating symbols according to agreed mathematical rules. The proof [that is, the query result] is as sound and consistent as the rules are. The First Order Predicate Calculus is sound and consistent" [2].

The numerous practical benefits of the theory have been detailed elsewhere [4]. To take advantage of them, databases and DBMSs must adhere to the pertinent mathematical and logical principles. For databases, one of the principles is that tables must have the properties of mathematical sets—they must obey **relational closure**. Sets have no duplicates or essential ordering, and, therefore, tables should not have them either (hence the mandatory key requirement, see Chapter 3). For DBMSs, another principle is that table operations (the derivation rules) must be logically sound. Both principles must be adhered to for the practical benefits to materialize.

Tables with duplicates do not have set properties. Those like the ones in Figure 4.1 have **list** properties and those like the ones in Figure 4.4 have **tuple-bag** properties. The operations for lists and tuple-bags differ from relational operations on sets and do not have as demonstrably a complete, consistent, and simple theoretical foundation as the dual relational one does [2]. Consequently, duplicates cause complications and practical problems, not all of which are obvious.

> ❖ **Note:** The difference between a list and a tuple-bag is that the former has *essential ordering*. Thus, "[the table in Figure 4.4] is more appropriate when the source of the data is as informative as a list can be [order is meaningful], while [that in the preceding note] might be preferred when the source is no more informative than a tuple-bag can be" [2].

4.3 Practical Implications

4.3.1 SQL and Duplicates

Keys in SQL are optional (see Chapter 3), and, therefore, if one is not defined for every table (and enforced by the DBMS), duplicates can inadvertently or intentionally occur, violating relational closure [4]. Nefarious implications can be demonstrated for most commercial SQL DBMSs, which "do permit duplicate rows, but lack an adequate mechanism for distinguishing between them and an adequate set of operators for dealing with them" [5].

4.3.1.1 Duplicate Removal

Inspection of SQL techniques for removing duplicates (see Appendix 4A) reveals that they all suffer from one or more of the following drawbacks:

- Nonlogical access with loss of **data independence** [4]
- Complexity
- Heavy resource consumption
- Proprietary nature

Duplicates must, of course, be detected before they can be deleted, which requires an additional step with similar drawbacks. Blind deletion of duplicates is risky. It is possible, for example, that two duplicates represent distinct entities in the real world, but if the database design fails to capture the attribute that distinguishes between them, they consequently become duplicates inadvertently. If so, deletion will result in loss of information. The solution is, of course, to add the distinguishing column to the table and update the other rows in the table accordingly. In transactional databases with large tables, an optimal trade-off point between duplicate tracking and removal (integrity) and resource consumption (performance) is not easy to choose.

4.3.1.2 Countability

Database rows are the outcome of a recording and entry process, which is prone to errors, including duplication errors. If duplicates are employed for representation, it is not possible to distinguish between "intentional" duplicates and duplication errors. The integrity of the database is lost because the number of rows does not necessarily reflect the actual number of entities in the real world. This is a direct consequence of countability being predicated on distinguishability—"we must consider individual [boxes] as entities . . . [we] need to distinguish them, even if just to count them" [3]. Counts in databases that contain duplicates are highly suspect.

4.3.1.3 Addressability

Just like the entities they represent, distinguishable rows are *self-identifying* and, thus, *addressable logically* via their distinguishing column(s). In the same manner in which actual boxes can be referred to as "this one" versus "that one" by pointing to their location in space, the distinct rows in Figure 4.2A can be addressed using the key column ITEM in the database, for example, ITEM 1 versus ITEM 2.

Individual duplicates on the other hand, are not addressable logically. Suppose there are N duplicate rows representing boxes in a supermarket database and one row needs to be deleted each time a box is sold.

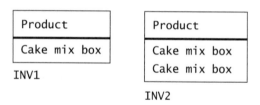

Figure 4.5. *Database with Duplicates*

Because duplicates are not self-identifying, how can only one of them be deleted (or, for that matter, updated) in SQL? Either all N rows must be deleted and N–1 rows reinserted, or some *nonlogical* addressing scheme (e.g., row order in physical storage) must be employed. Both approaches are cumbersome and resource consuming, yet either would have to be repeated for every box sale (see Appendix 4A). Note that these complications do not exist for the design in Figure 4.2B.

4.3.1.4 Correctness and Interpretability of Results

Figure 4.5 shows two tables representing inventories at two locations.

Consider the two SQL queries and their results shown in Figure 4.6. One operation—DISTINCT—deems duplicates indistinguishable, but another—COUNT()—does not. "[I]t is very unwise to have more than one criterion of identity unless each criterion is explicitly defined (and it is always 100 percent clear which one is being used, and, moreover, each one can be used in all contexts in which it makes sense). The criterion

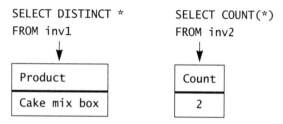

Figure 4.6. *Distinguishability under SQL*

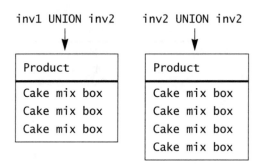

Figure 4.7. *UNION and Duplicates*

for the operator DISTINCT is explicitly defined (I suppose), but the criterion [for which COUNT(*)] deliver 2, rather than 1, is not defined" [2].

Consider also the queries and results shown in Figure 4.7.

> That the union of something to itself is not the very same thing [is] absurd . . . that the union of two collections can be smaller than both of them [is] . . . counterintuitive. [2]

Similar oddities can be demonstrated for all relational table operations. Appendix 4B shows that when nine syntactically different, but semantically equivalent SQL formulations are applied to tables with duplicates, they produce nine results that differ in the number of duplicates they contain. The question for the user is *what do these differences mean?* Can any one of the results be considered more "correct" than the others and if so, on what grounds? And if the differences do not mean anything, why produce different results in the first place, particularly with real-world complex databases, where interpretation of such results is practically impossible and performance is affected to boot (see Section 4.3.1.5).

4.3.1.5 Essential Order and Performance Optimization

SQL DBMSs are frequently criticized for poor performance, purportedly due to their relational nature. This is misguided, of course, because the relational model is purely logical and performance is determined at the *physical* level and is, therefore, a pure implementation matter. However, because adherence to relational principles facilitates system optimization, it is SQL's *violation* of those principles that inhibits it. Duplicates are a case in point.

SQL is a redundant language: The same query can be expressed in many ways, which means that semantically equivalent expressions can vary widely in performance [7]. In the absence of DBMS optimization, users must consider very carefully how to formulate their queries to avoid performance penalties, a burden that they are ill-equipped to handle and that relational technology was devised to eliminate. SQL's redundancy makes the development of optimizers difficult, so it would be beneficial if, at the very least, semantically equivalent SQL statements produced—as they well should—the same result. It would then be possible for optimizers to *transform* a user's expression into a better performing one prior to execution, relieving the user from the burden of performance considerations. But this relational benefit can only be achieved with *relational tables*, which don't have duplicates.

With duplicates, equivalent expressions do not produce the same result, but instead, results that differ in their number of duplicates (see Appendix 4A). Consequently "the system optimizer has to be extremely careful in its task of expression transformation . . . In other words, duplicate rows act as a significant optimization inhibitor . . . [with the following] implications:

- Optimizer code itself is harder to write, harder to maintain, and probably more buggy

- System performance is likely to be worse than it might otherwise be

- Users are going to have to get involved in performance issues. [8]

Consider, for example, the proprietary SQL extensions devised to handle hierarchic (tree) explosions, which produce results with *meaningfully ordered* duplicates, such as those in Figure 4.3. The order carries meaning because it reflects the tree location of the nodes represented by the rows. It is extremely desirable to further query such results, but SQL in general and those SQL dialects implementing the extensions in particular lack the proper relational operations that would produce the correct results. Consequently, explosion results cannot be further operated upon in SQL because relational operations eliminate duplicates (e.g., DISTINCT, UNION) and the information will be lost. One particular implementation (in the process of being incorporated into the SQL standard) uses the standard's nonrelational version of the UNION operation, UNION ALL, to preserve the duplicates in the result. Explosion operations are, therefore, severely limited and, what is more, perform badly because the SQL DBMS cannot allow the optimizer to reorder rows, if desirable for performance, to prevent information loss (see Chapter 7).

4.4 Conclusion and Recommendations

Duplicates produce a plethora of serious complications and problems yet offer no benefit. Arguments for duplicates simply do not withstand scrutiny. The practical complications they cause stem from violations of both theoretical foundations of the relational model:

- Logical confusion by users as to the entity types of interest and, therefore, the formulation and representation of propositions; clearly defined and identified entity types lead to properly formulated propositions, represented accurately by relational tables without duplicates.

- Mathematical mismatch by the data language, where nonset constructs, such as lists and tuple-bags are allowed, but operated upon with relational operators that are appropriate only for sets [5].

It makes no sense to accept the confusion and further complicate the data language with unsound, nonset functionality and lose the relational benefits, just to facilitate the removal of duplicates that need not and should not be in the database in the first place and can be easily prevented. Indeed, the absence of such facilitation in SQL is "a blessing in disguise since [it] effectively serve[s] as an incentive to users not to have duplicate rows in the first place" [3]. Unfortunately, judging from SQL's SELECT ALL and UNION ALL, the industry does not heed this principle.

The solution is, clearly, to prohibit duplicates. Users would do well to define a key—even if a surrogate—for each and every table and use DISTINCT whenever appropriate to ensure that results do not contain duplicates.

> ❖ **Note:** The nonrelational, tuple-bag SQL operators, UNION ALL and SELECT ALL, preserve duplicates in results. Interestingly "SELECT DISTINCT takes longer to execute than SELECT ALL, in general, even if DISTINCT is effectively a no-operation instruction . . . that [is] because always eliminating duplicates appears to imply performance problems, [so] the SQL language designers had a strong motivation to make not eliminating duplicates the default" [6].

As to objections to arbitrary keys, such as, for example:

> *The row ["Cake mix box,1.10"] could appear three times [on a*
> *supermarket checkout receipt] with a significance that would not escape*

> *many shoppers . . . [insofar as it] is useful to record the information,*
> *there are no value components that distinguish the objects. What the*
> *relational model does is force people to often invent meaningless values*
> *to be inserted in an extra column, whose purpose is to show what we*
> *knew already, that the [boxes] are distinct.*
>   —TRADE PUBLICATION ARTICLE

a checkout receipt is a *report* and, as an *application*, does not have to
include the key. Duplicates do not cause problems for receipts, but can
sure wreak havoc with inventories. Besides, users would not have to
"invent" keys if the DBMS generated them on its own (see Chapter 3).
This is particularly true for databases representing hierarchies (trees),
where multiple keys may be necessary (see Chapter 7).

References

[1] E. F. Codd, presentation, 1970.

[2] H. Darwen, "The Duplicity of Duplicate Rows," *Relational Database Writings 1989–1991*, Reading, MA: Addison-Wesley, 1992.

[3] F. Pascal, *Understanding Relational Databases*, New York, NY: John Wiley & Sons, 1993.

[4] F. Pascal, *Understanding Relational Databases*, New York, NY: John Wiley & Sons, 1993.

[5] C. J. Date, "And Cauldron Bubble," *Database Programming and Design*, June 1995.

[6] C. J. Date, "Toil and Trouble," *Relational Database Writings 1991–1994*, Reading, MA: Addison-Wesley, 1995.

[7] F. Pascal, "SQL Redundancy and DBMS Performance," *Database Programming and Design*, December 1988.

Duplicate Removal in SQL

The following duplicate removal methods from various sources were not checked for accuracy, completeness, applicability to, or compatibility with specific SQL DBMSs. The purpose is only to illustrate the general nature and implications of such methods. Some have one statement, others are multistatement procedures. For reasons explained in the chapter, duplicates should be reviewed prior to deletion. Steps for *detecting* duplicates for review are not always included. All notes other than comments come from the method's source.

Method 1

```
DELETE
FROM boxes
WHERE description
  NOT IN
    (SELECT MIN(description)
     FROM boxes
     GROUP BY description)
  AND price NOT IN
       (SELECT MIN(price)
         FROM boxes
         GROUP BY price);
```

Comments: With duplicates there is no minimum value; the procedure arbitrarily removes whichever of the duplicates is selected *first* by the DBMS. Implicit reliance is on row order and on the DBMS removing the first selected row, even though all selected rows have the same values, which not all DBMSs may do. This is likely to be slow with very large tables.

Method 2

This procedure eliminates duplicate rows inexpensively from very large tables. With large rollbacks, if rollback segments cause problems in steps 3 or 4, add a PL*SQL block with a COMMIT at every nnK row in the step. This procedure can be scheduled for off hours. Step 4 should normally be a very fast step.

```
/* step 1
/* create a non-unique index on the columns in
/* question.
/* eliminates need for DBMS to store column sets for
/* comparison, or do multiple table scans
/* allows the query to scan just the index
CREATE INDEX xdups
ON boxes (description,price)
TABLESPACE temp
PCTFREE 1
STORAGE ... * *
PARALLEL xx
/* step 2
/* review duplicates
/* creates mirror table to hold the duplicates which
/* adds the base table ROWID as column (here, first)
CREATE TABLE dups
  AS (SELECT a.ROWID row_id, a.*
      FROM boxes a
      WHERE 1=2);
/* step 3
/* populate mirror table
/* all duplicates except the row with the lowest rowid will be
   inserted
```

```
/* the lowest ROWID row can be included with minor
/* change, but be careful on the DELETE step
INSERT INTO dups
SELECT a.ROWID, a.*
FROM boxes a
WHERE a.rowid > (SELECT MIN(b.ROWID)
                 FROM boxes b
                 WHERE a.description = b.description
                   AND a.price=b.price);
/* step 4
/* delete duplicates
DELETE
FROM boxes a
WHERE a.rowid IN
                (SELECT row_id
                 FROM dupe);
```

Comments: This is a complex, highly procedural solution with physical exposure and loss of data independence. ROWID is a physical pointer and PL*SQL is a language proprietary to the specific DBMS, and, thus, the procedure cannot be used with other DBMSs. It involves the user in performance issues.

Method 3

Keep running the DELETE operation until the DBMS says zero rows deleted because if there are three or more duplicates it deletes only one.

```
/* find and remove duplicates
DELETE
FROM boxes
WHERE (ROWID,description,price)
  IN (SELECT MAX(ROWID),description,price
      FROM boxes
      GROUP BY description,price
      HAVING COUNT(*) > 1);
```

Comments: A variant of procedure 2, this one also relies on ROWID. The procedure needs to be looped to remove multiple duplicates.

Method 4

```
/* step 1
/* create copy of table without the duplicates
CREATE TABLE newboxes
  AS SELECT DISTINCT *
    FROM boxes;
/* step 2
/* drop original table
DROP boxes;
/* step 3
/* rename new table to old table
ALTER TABLE newboxes
RENAME TO boxes;
```

Comments: This is a relatively simple procedure, but very expensive with very large tables. The DBMS must support a RENAME clause for ALTER TABLE.

Method 5

```
DELETE
FROM boxes t1
WHERE EXISTS
    (SELECT *
     FROM boxes t2
     WHERE t2.description = t1.description
       AND t2.price = t1.price
       AND t2.ROWID > t1.ROWID);
```

Comments: This is another ROWID variant, using a self-join.

Method 6

```
/* sort table in index order
/* operation deletes duplicates
CREATE CLUSTERED INDEX xdups
ON boxes (description,price)
WITH IGNORE_DUP_KEY
```

Comments: This is another nonlogical, proprietary variant, which is expensive with large tables.

■ ■ ■ ■ ■ ■ ■ ■ ■ ■ # 4B

Language Redundancy and Duplicates

This example is for illustration purposes only. Upon completion of this book the reader should recognize that the table and query design are questionable. But then, *any* design that involves duplicates is questionable by definition. The problem is exacerbated by language redundancy—the ability to express the same query in many different ways is a SQL—a flaw separate from allowing duplicates, which has its own drawbacks [1]. The queries and results were verified against a widely used SQL DBMS. However

> [If you] try out the nine formulations and any others you can think of on your own DBMS, [y]ou might discover some interesting things about your optimizer. Incidentally, . . . [there are] certainly products that do not handle the degree of duplication correctly in all cases— presumably because they are making some expression transformations that are technically incorrect. [2]

Given the two tables

Product	Description
CM1	Cake mix box
CM1	Cake mix box
CM1	Cake mix box
CM2	Cake mix box

PRODUCTS

Supplier	Product
S1	CM1
S1	CM1
S1	CM2

SUPPLY

the following nine alternative SQL formulations of the query "What are the products that are either cake mix boxes, or are supplied by supplier S1, or both?" yield nine answers that differ only in the number of duplicates they contain.

❖ **Note:** The DESCRIPTION column in the PRODUCTS table is not a key; that is, there are multiple types of cake mix boxes (CM1, CM2).

Expression 1

```
SELECT product
FROM products
WHERE description='Cake mix box'
  OR product IN
            (SELECT product
             FROM supply
             WHERE supplier='s1');
```

PRODUCT
CM1
CM1
CM1
CM2

Expression 2

```
SELECT product
FROM supply
WHERE supplier='s1'
  OR product IN
            (SELECT product
             FROM products
             WHERE description='Cake mix box');
```

PRODUCT
CM1
CM1
CM2

Expression 3

```
SELECT p.product
FROM products p,supply s
WHERE (s.supplier='s1'
 AND p.product=s.product)
    OR p.description='Cake mix box';
```

PRODUCT
CM1
CM1
CM1
CM2
CM1
CM1
CM1
CM2
CM1
CM1
CM1
CM2

Expression 4

```
SELECT supply.product
FROM products p,supply s
WHERE (s.supplier='s1'
  AND p.product=s.product)
    OR p.description='Cake mix box';
```

PRODUCT
CM1
CM1
CM1
CM1
CM1
CM1
CM1
CM1
CM2
CM2
CM2
CM2

Expression 5

```
SELECT product
FROM products
WHERE description='Cake mix box'
UNION ALL
SELECT product
FROM supply
WHERE supplier='s1';
```

PRODUCT
CM1
CM1
CM1
CM2
CM1
CM1
CM2

Expression 6

```
SELECT DISTINCT product
FROM products
WHERE description='Cake mix box'
UNION ALL
SELECT product
FROM supply
WHERE supplier='s1';
```

PRODUCT
CM1
CM2
CM1
CM1
CM2

Expression 7

```
SELECT product
FROM products
WHERE description='Cake mix box'
UNION ALL
SELECT DISTINCT product
FROM supply
WHERE supplier='s1';
```

PRODUCT
CM1
CM1
CM1
CM2
CM1
CM2

Expression 8

```
SELECT p.product
FROM products p,supply s
GROUP BY p.product,p.description,s.supplier,s.product
HAVING (s.supplier='s1'
  AND p.product=s.product)
    OR p.description='Cake mix box';
```

PRODUCT
CM1
CM1
CM2
CM2

Expression 9

```
SELECT product
FROM products
WHERE description='Cake mix box'
UNION
SELECT DISTINCT product
FROM supply
WHERE supplier='s1';
```

PRODUCT
CM1
CM2

References

[1] F. Pascal, "SQL Redundancy and DBMS Performance," *Database Programming and Design,* December 1988.

[2] C. J. Date, "Toil and Trouble," *Relational Database Writings 1991–1994,* Reading, MA: Addison-Wesley, 1995.

5

The Key, the Whole Key, and Nothing but the Key: Normalization

The relational model states that in order to be in 1NF [First Normal Form], a table can have no repeating groups. But since SQL does not support repeating groups, the only way] people can write a repeating group in SQL . . . is

```
CREATE TABLE employee
(emp# INTEGER PRIMARY KEY,
ename CHAR(15) NOT NULL,
child1 CHAR(15),
child2 CHAR(15),
: :
child5 CHAR(15))
```
—TRADE PUBLICATION ARTICLE

I'll need to "de-normalize" if I want to get any performance.
—TRADE PUBLICATION ARTICLE

Complex structure can be represented directly without the need to normalize.
—TRADE PUBLICATION ARTICLE

5.1 The Issue

Despite the fact that they were repeatedly debunked, arguments against normalization and for denormalization continue to sway practitioners, be they experienced or novices. This costs dearly and reveals the poor understanding of sound database principles by even those who profess to be experts in the field. It is both a major reason for and a consequence of deficiencies in SQL implementations and for technology regressions, such as ODBMS and OLAP, that have come to haunt SQL DBMSs.

This chapter

- Explains the principles behind normalization

- Demonstrates the advantages of adhering to them and the drawbacks of violating them

- Clarifies normalization levels and illustrates the procedures for achieving them

- Assesses performance and integrity implications for databases in general and SQL databases in particular

- Draws conclusions and offers some recommendations

Integrity complications caused by redundancy stemming from denormalized tables as well as other reasons are illustrated in detail in Chapter 8.

5.2 Fundamentals

Logically, a database table represents a set of true propositions about real-world entities of interest. Tables representing propositions about entities *of one type* are said to be fully normalized. For example, the rows in Figure 5.1 represent propositions about employees—entities of type Employee.

> ❖ **Note:** Loosely, a base table can be viewed as representing an entity type, defined as the collection of all attributes of interest of entities with regard to that type.

EMP#	ENAME	DEPT#	HIREDATE	SALARY
100	Spenser	E21	06-19-1980	26150
110	Lucchessi	A00	05-16-1958	38170
120	O'Connell	A00	12-05-1963	37950
130	Quintana	C01	07-28-1971	33800
140	Nicholls	C01	12-15-1976	35420
150	Adamson	D11	02-12-1972	30280
160	Pianka	D11	10-11-1977	27250
290	Parker	D31	05-30-1980	15340
310	Setright	D31	09-12-1964	15900

Figure 5.1. *Fully Normalized Table*

If, however, tables are designed such that they "bundle" multiple entity types, certain complications ensue—redundancy and update anomalies—which increase the potential for database inconsistencies. This imposes on users and the DBMS the burden of additional integrity constraints that need to be declared and enforced to guarantee consistency and, thus, correctness of the database and query results. The additional constraints are unnecessary if a table represents (propositions about) entities of one type.

Note very carefully that *correct and complete* mapping of a conceptual (business) model to a **logical model** will always yield fully normalized tables. It is only if and when poor design has bundled multiple entity types into single tables that those tables must undergo an explicit process of **normalization**. In other words, normalization is a *re*design process that unbundles the entity types and eliminates the complications. The process involves decomposition without loss of information of the poorly designed tables via projection operations into multiple tables such that each represents only one entity type and is, therefore, fully normalized.

There are several kinds of bundling, each requiring a normalization (unbundling) procedure of its own. The procedures form a hierarchy, whereby a normalization procedure higher in the hierarchy yields tables in a higher **normal form** (NF), that is, further normalized, with less inconsistency risk and integrity burdens.

5.2.1 Repeating Groups

In some old prerelational data files or databases, many-to-one (M:1) relationships between entities of different types were represented by **repeating groups**. For example, in the first employee-children example at the beginning of the chapter, there are two entity types, employees and children, and the logical relationship between them would be described hierarchically as follows

```
EMPLOYEE
   emp#
   ename
   CHILDREN
      cname1
      cage1
      cname2
      cage2
       :
```

where CHILDREN is a repeating group: For each "parent" record (EMPLOYEE) there is a group of child fields (CNAME,CAGE) that repeats as many times as an employee has children. If the group consists of only one field, for example, CNAME, it reduces to a **repeating field**.

> [Repeating groups] . . . consist of a fixed part, namely the [employee name] and a varying part, namely the set of [child] entries (... varying in the sense that the number of entries it contains—varies from one [employee] record to another) . . . the hierarchic record type consists of [two] single employee fields and a repeating group of child information . . . which consists of [single child fields]. [1]

In older, hierarchic databases, the stored records would look like the ones in Figure 5.2 (the third employee does not have any children, but the others do). There were usually **physical pointers** from the parent record to the child records. The pointers were exposed to users in applications in the sense that the pointers needed to be explicitly "navigated" during database access to obtain the desired information.

For both simplicity and **data independence**, the relational approach did away with pointers [2]. In a table-based database, all information—relationships included—is represented *logically*, only as values in tables. The equivalent of a repeating group in such a database would be a **multivalued column**. Figure 5.3 shows an unnormalized table, with the multivalued column CHILDREN representing the repeating field CNAME.

Tables with multivalued columns represent mixtures of entity types (more precisely, their rows represent propositions about entities of multiple types), here, employees and children. Some deficiencies of such designs are obvious:

- Possibility that the preset number of times the group repeats (here, five) will not be sufficient (if an employee has six or more children)

- Waste of storage space for employees who have fewer than five or no children

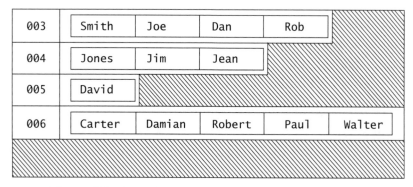

Figure 5.2. *Stored Repeating Field Hierarchic Database*

EMP#	ENAME	CHILDREN
003	Smith	Joe
		David
		Rob
004	Jones	Jim
		Jean
005	David	
006	Carter	Damian
		Roberta
		Paul
		Walter

Figure 5.3. *Unnormalized Table*

But if a DBMS has *explicit* support of multivalued columns, additional, less obvious complications will arise [3]:

- *More complex addressing scheme.* The combination 'table name + column name + key value' will no longer be unique for every value and, thus, would not be sufficient to address logically each and every database value.

- *Increase in the number of necessary data operations.* For single-valued columns, at least four operations must be supported by the data language: insert, retrieve, update, and delete. But with multivalued columns, there must be two versions of these operations, one for single-valued and another for multivalued columns, doubling the number of operations.

- *Increased operation complexity.* Operations on multivalued columns must rely on the *order* of values within the column, and order-based operations are notoriously complex and prone to errors. (For the reader familiar with arrays, the addressing of values within the column and, thus, data operations, must rely on subscripts.)

- *More complex queries.* Some queries are difficult to express, for example, "Who are the employees who have two children, Steve and Roberta?"

- *Lack of formal design guidelines.* "If the system supports repeating groups, we now have multiple ways of representing the same information (at the very least we can do it with and without repeating groups; there are probably several variants with repeating groups). Which design will we follow? How do we design? Is there any scientific basis (like the principles of further normalization) for making such decisions?" [3]

First Normal Form.   Multivalued columns produce complications and provide no benefits. In fact, "There is nothing that can be represented logically with repeating groups that cannot also be represented without them" [4]. The information in the table in Figure 5.3, for example, can be represented by two tables with single-valued columns, shown in Figure 5.4. Note that each of these two tables represents propositions about entities of one type.

Tables without multivalued columns are in **first normal form** (1NF), or normalized. The relational model requires all database tables to be in 1NF, so relational tables are normalized by definition.

> ❖ **Note:** There is nothing to prevent users from encoding multiple values in one column. All a DBMS can do is discourage such designs by not providing explicit special operators and integrity support for them (see Chapter 3).

EMP#	CNAME
003	Joe
003	David
003	Rob
004	Jim
004	Jean
006	Carter
006	Damian
006	Roberta
006	Paul
006	Walter

EMP#	ENAME
003	Smith
004	Jones
005	Davies
006	Carter

EMPLOYEES   CHILDREN

Figure 5.4. *1NF (Normalized) Tables*

5.2.2 Column Dependencies

A dependency exists between two columns in a table if the values in one column are associated with the values of another column.

Note, first, that if a table represents (propositions about) entities of one type, all columns represent attributes of entities of that type. And due to the fact that entities represented by rows are *identified* by key values, it can be said that all columns are "about the key." Thus, in Figure 5.1 the EMPLOYEES table represents entities of type Employees, and columns ENAME, DEPT#, HIREDATE, and SALARY are all "about"—that is, functionally dependent on—EMP#.

Second, a dependency relationship between columns is, essentially, an integrity constraint on the values of the dependent column, representing a business rule in the real world (see Chapter 2); it constrains the values of the dependent column to conform with the dependency. When a table represents one entity type, the only dependencies are those of *nonkey columns on the key column(s)*. If the **key constraint**, uniqueness, is enforced, key values will never repeat and, thus, neither will the dependent nonkey values, which means there will be no redundancy due to dependency (see Chapter 3). In other words, with fully normalized tables, enforcing the key constraint is *all* that is required to guarantee no redundancy and no inconsistencies. Conversely, in tables that are not fully normalized— that is, tables that represent mixed entity types—dependencies are not on the key, or not *directly* on the key, or not on the *whole* key and, therefore

- Entities of one type cannot be added or dropped *independently* of entities of another type, causing possible **insert/delete anomalies**.

- Values of the independent columns are not unique; they can repeat and cause the dependent values to repeat, causing redundancy (see Chapter 8) and thus potential **update anomalies**.

In such cases, the key constraint is not sufficient to prevent redundancy and database inconsistencies.

Unless entity types are separated in distinct tables, the integrity of dependencies not on the key, the whole key, or nothing but the key can be guaranteed only by declaring *additional constraints* necessary to enforce such dependencies. The purpose of the process of **further normalization** beyond 1NF is to unbundle the entity types and obviate the need for the additional integrity burden. Full normalization also makes the database easier to understand and query.

There are several types of column dependencies. The correct design rules, or the further normalization (redesign) rules to eliminate those dependencies, are governed by **dependency theory** [5].

> ❖ **Note:** Dependency theory formalizes what is rather intuitive to knowl-
> edgeable database designers. It is "nothing more than formalized common
> sense. [But] the whole point of the theory underlying this area is to try and
> identify common sense principles and formalize them . . . then we can
> mechanize [them] . . . write a program and get the machine to do the work
> [enforce integrity] . . . critics of normalization usually miss this point; they
> claim (quite rightly) that the ideas are all basically common sense, but they
> typically do not realize that it is a significant achievement to state what
> 'common sense' means in a precise and formal way" [1].

5.2.2.1 Functional Dependencies

A **functional dependency** (FD) between two columns exists when values in one column are associated with values in another column [5].

Second Normal Form.   If all columns are functionally dependent on the
whole key (not just a part thereof) as in Figure 5.1, a table is in **second
normal form** (2NF).

Consider table A in Figure 5.5 in light of the following business rules in
the real world

- Staffing is on a per project activity (activities within projects) basis.

- Managers and their departments are assigned to projects.

The table does not have multivalued columns and is, therefore, normalized (in 1NF). But note the highlighted association of PMGR# and
DEPT# values with PROJ# values. PROJ# is only *part of the key*. The
association reflects the bundling of two entity types, projects and activities: Although STAFF is functionally dependent on the whole
composite key (it is an activity attribute), PMGR# and DEPT# are

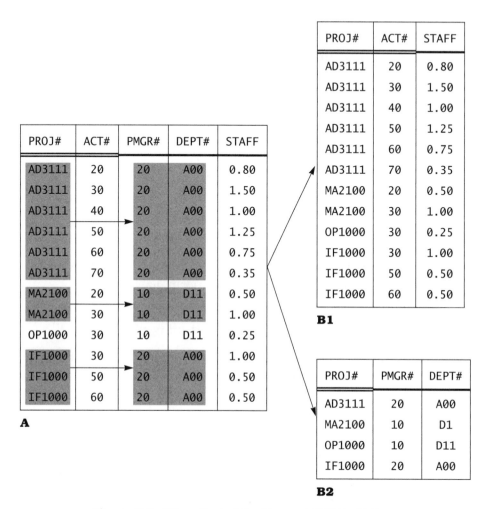

Figure 5.5. *FD on Part of the Key and 2NF Projections*

attributes of projects and, thus, functionally dependent on the key component PROJ#. Formally

```
{PROJ#,ACT#} -> STAFF
PROJ# -> {PMGR#, DEPT#}
```

This type of FD causes the following complications:

- Information about new managers assigned to projects that do not yet have activities cannot be inserted into the table.

- Deleting information about the sole activity of a project also deletes the information about the project manager.

- Redundancy—PROJ# values repeat causing their dependent PMGR# and DEPT# values to repeat; thus, when the manager of a project changes, the rows of all activities of that project must be updated.

If such designs are not avoided, an additional integrity constraint is necessary besides the key constraint to guarantee consistency (see Chapter 8). This can be avoided by further normalization, namely decomposition that separates the FDs into two projections whose non-key columns are dependent on the whole key and, therefore, are in 2NF.

The two 2NF projections of A, B1, and B2 are shown in Figure 5.5. The original table can be recovered without any information loss by joining the two projections.

Third Normal Form.   If all columns are functionally dependent *directly* on the whole key, as in Figure 5.1, a table is in **third normal form** (3NF).

Consider projection B2 in the previous example, shown as table A in Figure 5.6, and assume the following business rule in the real world:

- Departments are assigned to project managers;

- Project managers are assigned to projects;

All nonkey columns are dependent on the whole key and, consequently, the table is in 2NF. But note the highlighted association of DEPT# values with PMGR# values. It reflects the bundling of two entity types, projects and departments: Although PMGR# is functionally

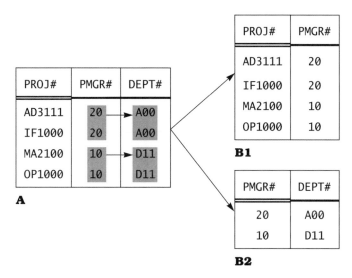

Figure 5.6. *Indirect FD on the Key and 3NF Projections*

dependent directly on the key PROJ# (it represents an attribute of projects), DEPT# is directly dependent on PMGR#, a *nonkey* column and, thus, only indirectly dependent on the key (it represents an attribute of project managers). Formally, departments are *transitively* (indirectly) dependent on projects via the project managers' direct dependency on projects:

PROJ# -> PMGR# -> DEPT#

This type of FD causes the following complications:

- Information about new managers that are not yet assigned to projects cannot be inserted into the table.

- Deleting information about the sole project of a manager also deletes the information about the manager.

- Redundancy—PMGR# values repeat causing DEPT# values to repeat; when the department of a manager changes, all rows of that project manager must be updated.

If such designs are not avoided, an additional integrity constraint is necessary besides the key constraint to guarantee consistency (see Chapter 8). This can be avoided by further normalization, namely decomposition that separates the FDs into two projections whose nonkey columns are directly dependent on the key and, therefore, are in 3NF.

```
PROJ# -> PMGR#
PMGR# -> DEPT#
```

The two 3NF projections of A, B1, and B2 are shown in Figure 5.6. The original table can be recovered without any information loss by joining the two projections.

3NF tables with a simple key (one column) are devoid of redundancy and update anomalies *due to FDs,* which means that for such tables—the majority—3NF means full normalization. Tables in 3NF with composite keys (see Chapter 3) can still suffer from complications due to other types of column dependency and require further normalization to eliminate them.

❖ **Note:** A special—and rare—case is that of composite candidate keys that *overlap,* for example,

```
RESERVE {ROOM#,ARR_DATE,DPT_DATE,...}
```

where {ROOM#,ARR_DATE} and {ROOM#,DPT_DATE} are candidate keys. Even though such tables are in 3NF, they suffer from additional redundancies and update anomalies [1]. A normal form stronger than 3NF—**Boyce-Codd normal form** (BCNF)—generalizes 3NF to cover such tables. They are decomposed via projections into tables that are in BCNF.

```
ARRIVALS {ROOM#,ARR_DATE,...}
DEPARTS {ROOM#,DPT_DATE,...}
```

A simple surrogate key (e.g., RES#) is advisable in such cases (see Chapter 3)

5.2.2.2 Multivalued Dependencies

A **multivalued dependency** (MVD) between two columns exists when *sets* of values in one column are each associated with values in another column. MVDs are dependencies among parts of a composite key and are a more general form of dependency than FDs: all FDs are MVDs, but not all MVDs are FDs [1]. Like FDs, MVDs cause similar complications, but they are somewhat less intuitive.

Fourth Normal Form.   If no multivalued dependencies exist between columns, a table is in **fourth normal form** (4NF).

The table in Figure 5.7 represents assignments of employees to projects and activities. Assume the following business rules in the real world:

- An employee can be assigned to any project and, within those projects, to all activities.

- An employee can be assigned to the same activities regardless of project assignments (assignments to projects and activities are independent).

- A project or activity can have any number of employees assigned to it.

The rules mean that the relationships between employees, projects, and activities are each many-to-many (M:M), and that projects and

EMP#	PROJ	ACT
130	Query Services	DEBUG
	User Education	SUPP
30	Query Services	DEBUG
		TEST
		CODE

Figure 5.7. *MVDs—The Unnormalized Representation*

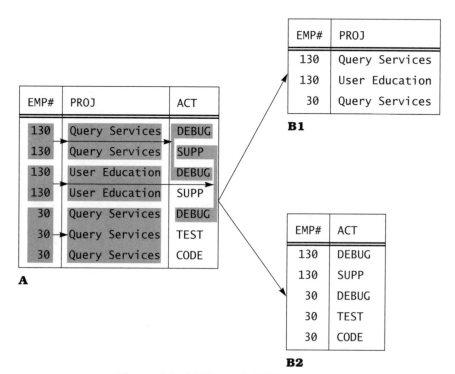

Figure 5.8. *MVDs and 4NF Projections*

activities may repeat for each employee. The design in Figure 5.7 has the table equivalent of repeating groups—multivalued columns—and the table is, therefore, not in 1NF, which has already been shown in a previous section to cause complications.

To normalize the design, the table must be "flattened" in order to eliminate the multivalued columns (M:M relationships must be split into two M:1 relationships). The 1NF result is table A in Figure 5.8 with the composite key {EMP#,PROJ,ACT}. But because all columns are components of the key, there are no nonkey columns, and, thus, no FDs on nonkey columns, so the table is also in 3NF. Note, however, the highlighted association of *sets* of PROJ and ACT values with EMP# values. These *intra-key* dependencies reflect the bundling of two entity types, employee project assignment and employee activity assignment. Formally, PROJ and ACT, parts of the key, are *multivalued dependent* on EMP#, another part of the key.

```
EMP# ->> PROJ
EMP# ->> ACT
```

This type of dependency causes the following complications:

- Information about new project assignments of employees who are not yet assigned to activities cannot be inserted into the table.

- Deleting information about the sole project assignment of an employee also deletes the information about activity assignment.

- Redundancy—EMP# values repeat causing sets of PROJ and ACT values to repeat and thus, when the project assignment, or the activity assignment of an employee changes, the rows of all project or all activity assignments of that employee must be updated.

If such designs are not avoided, an additional integrity constraint is necessary besides the key constraint to guarantee consistency (see Chapter 8). This can be avoided by further normalization, namely decomposition that separates the MVDs into two projections whose columns have no intra-key dependencies and, therefore, are in 4NF.

The 4NF projections of A, B1, and B2 are shown in Figure 5.7. The original table can be recovered without information loss by joining the two projections.

5.2.2.3 Join Dependencies

Join dependencies (JD) are a more general kind of MVD: All MVDs are JDs, but not all JDs are MVDs [1]. Like FDs and MVDs, JDs cause similar complications that are even less intuitive than MVDs.

Fifth Normal Form.   If there are no join dependencies between columns, a table is in **fifth normal form** (5NF).

Table A in Figure 5.9 representing assignments has the same structure, but not the same content, as Table A in Figure 5.8. Consider it in light of a different business rule regarding project and activity assignments, namely, the assignments are no longer independent of one another.

If employee E works for project P and project P has activity A and employee E is assigned to activity A, then employee E works for project P.

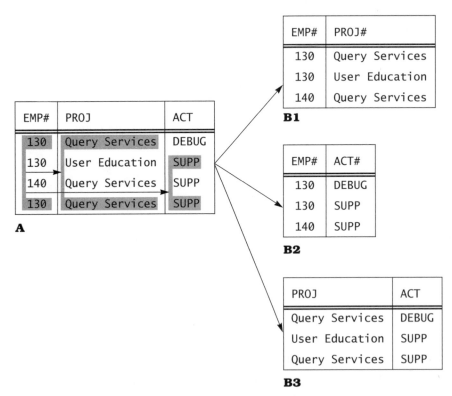

Figure 5.9. *Join Dependencies and Fifth Normal Form Projections*

> ❖ **Note:** Although it may seem that this rule is always in effect in such cir-
> cumstances—an assumption referred to as the **connection trap**—that is
> not necessarily the case. For example, it is possible that an employee is
> assigned to project P1; that project P1 has activity A1; that the employee is
> assigned to activity A1; but the employee is *not* assigned to *activity A1 in
> project P1*, but rather to some other activity A2 in project P1 and to activity
> A1 in some other project P2 [1]. Rules cannot be *assumed*, even when they
> seem plausible, but rather identified during the business modeling process.

The table in Figure 5.9 is in 4NF because there are no MVDs. But note
the highlighted association between EMP# and PROJ values and
between EMP# and ACT values. This reflects the following intra-key
JDs between key parts. Formally

```
{EMP#,PROJ#,ACT#} JD {EMP#,PROJ#}
{EMP#,PROJ#,ACT#} JD {PROJ#,ACT#}
{EMP#,PROJ#,ACT#} JD {EMP#,ACT#}
```

Such bundling produces redundancy and anomalies similar to those in
the preceding cases.

If such designs are not avoided, an additional integrity constraint is necessary besides the key constraint to guarantee consistency (see Chapter
8). This can be avoided by further normalization, namely decomposition
that separates the MVDs into projections—here, three—whose columns
have no intra-key dependencies and, therefore, are in 5NF.

The three 5NF projections of A, B1, B2, and B3 are shown in Figure
5.9. The original table can be recovered without information loss by
joining the three projections pairwise—two projections at a time ([B1
join B2] join B3).

Tables in 5NF are fully normalized—they suffer from no redundancies
or update anomalies *due to column dependencies* (Chapter 8 discusses
redundancies due to other reasons).

5.3 Practical Implications

5.3.1 SQL and Multivalued Columns

With respect to repeating groups, no DBMS can prevent users from designing tables with columns with multiple values, such as the one in Figure 5.2. A DBMS can only discourage their use by not providing *explicit* support—operations and integrity features—for multivalued columns. SQL DBMSs do not provide such support (although some use multivalued columns in their database catalogs).

Tables such as that produced by the SQL CREATE TABLE statement at the beginning of the chapter and shown in Figure 5.10, are different from the one in Figure 5.2 and, therefore, are not "the only way people can write a repeating group in SQL." The true equivalent to repeating groups in SQL tables is the multivalued column. Designs, such as the one in Figure 5.10, attempt to emulate repeating groups, so as to avoid the drawbacks of multivalued columns *without normalization*. But this trick does not eliminate all deficiencies caused by entity type bundling, for example, the difficulty to express certain queries.

With respect to dependencies, taking all the pertinent business rules into consideration is an integral part of business modeling (see Chapter 2). Correct identification and interpretation of those rules will implicitly produce fully normalized tables and, thus, avoid redundancies

EMP#	ENAME	CNAME1	CNAME2	CNAME3	CNAME4	CNAME5
003	Smith	Joe	David	Rob		
004	Jones	Jim	Jean			
005	David					
006	Carter	Damian	Roberta	Paul	Walter	

Figure 5.10. *Repeating Group Emulation without Multivalued Columns*

and anomalies. Consistency can then be guaranteed by the DBMS via enforcement of just key integrity constraints, which, implementation deficiencies notwithstanding, SQL DBMSs do support (see Chapter 3). Otherwise put, fully normalized tables are nothing but properly designed tables. Denormalized tables, on the other hand, are the result of poor design: They extend the integrity burden, unnecessarily increasing the risk of inconsistency in SQL systems, where the expression of nonkey integrity constraints can be prohibitively complex (see Chapters 2 and 8).

5.3.2 "Denormalization" and Performance

If less than fully normalized designs cause problems and offer no benefits, why is "denormalization" advocated for tables that were correctly designed in the first place [7]? Fully normalized designs provoke strenuous objections mainly for performance reasons. Many, if not most, practitioners, be they novices or experienced professionals, think that with information distributed in more tables, queries trying to assemble it must perform joins, which are disk I/O intensive and, thus, slow down performance. Bundling related information in a smaller number of denormalized tables avoids joins and, purportedly, improves performance. This fallacious—and costly—notion has been reinforced over time by three major industry factors.

First, SQL DBMSs do not achieve data independence—a clean separation between the logical and physical levels of representation—because they fail to provide sufficient flexibility in terms of physical design options (storage and access methods, optimization algorithms, concurrency mechanisms) to optimize performance to the maximum possible, and they fail to insulate the logical level from physical details. Implementing keys via indexes is a case in point; another is that only base tables can be physically stored. Therefore, joins require more disk I/Os *only when the joined tables are base tables.* If the *joins themselves* could be physically stored (which some products allow in the form of

clustered tables, for example), disk I/O would be reduced for *logical* joins. Otherwise put, it is the *physical implementation* of the DBMS that slows down performance, not the *logical* normalization of tables.

Second, despite the fact that the whole point of a centralized database is to be *application-neutral*, that is, to serve multiple applications equally well, database designers tend to take a narrow, application-specific perspective. With many applications running against the database, varying in pattern of access, there are inherent performance trade-offs. The more obvious are those between retrievals and updates: The redundancy caused by bundling (see Chapter 8) requires applying updates in more than one place, slowing them down. But there are also the less obvious trade-offs between different kinds of retrieval: bundling forces applications that do not need to access all the bundled information to read wider tables than necessary, which slows them down [3,7]. Even if bundling minimizes joins and disk I/O—and, as we shall see shortly, that is not necessarily the case—at best this biases the database for some applications, but against others [3].

Third, denormalization advocates simply ignore the *integrity implications* of the redundancy and update anomalies caused by it, which can be prohibitive in SQL systems (see Chapter 8). With denormalized databases, either additional integrity constraints are declared by users and enforced by the DBMS—assuming it was designed to do it—or there will be inconsistencies. The risk for the latter imposes on users the burden of declaring these constraints (with the accompanying error-proneness), and on the DBMS the burden of checking them in the catalog (which has a negative effect of its own on performance). In practice, the necessary constraints are simply ignored either out of unawareness or because they are too much trouble. The consequences, as put by one practitioner, are disastrous:

> *Finished testing a COBOL program for a software company whose main product is a well-known government contract accounting system . . . Now the [expletive deleted] database . . . is replete with repeating groups,*

redundant fields, etc. On top of all that, because it is one of the central files to the entire system, there are literally hundreds of rules and relationships, all of which must be enforced by the dozens of subprograms that access it. I found so many violations of so many of these rules in this new subprogram that I filled five single-spaced pages with comments and suggestions. And I probably missed [the more obscure problems]. Several [such problems], perhaps.

—Online message

❖ **Note:** Confusion of the logical and physical levels abounds in the industry and is the underlying source of many erroneous database practices, including denormalization. Instructive in this respect is the following criticism of this section by a reviewer of this book's manuscript.

Comments sometimes contradict each other. The author, for example, writes about denormalization: "Bundling related information in a smaller number of tables purportedly minimizes joins and, therefore, improves performance. This fallacious and costly notion . . ." After labeling the notion fallacious and implying that it is inaccurate, the author goes on to say: "It is the physical implementation of the DBMS that slows down performance" and implies that denormalization, in the real world, does improve performance.

There is no contradiction. Performance is determined entirely at the physical level, and logical normalization cannot possibly have any effect on it. Therefore, if performance problems arise in practice, they have nothing to do with normalization per se and everything to do with the physical implementation of the DBMS and/or the physical design of the database. It is, therefore, fallacious to argue that "denormalization enhances performance." If denormalization appears to improve performance in some (though by no means all) circumstances, it is only because SQL DBMSs have chosen to store only base tables and offer insufficient physical optimization options. The correct solution to the problem is not, therefore, to "denormalize for performance" and incur enormous integrity penalties (see Chapter 8) for questionable gains, but to improve DBMS implementations and *avoid* prohibitive integrity burdens and the high risk of inconsistent data.

5.4 Conclusion and Recommendations

There are many advantages to full normalization, not the least of which is that it produces databases that are easier to understand [8]. Bundling entity types into denormalized tables makes it more difficult to know where specific information resides in the database and express queries to obtain it. Deviations from fully normalized designs

- Increase inconsistency risks and integrity burdens

- Provide questionable benefits (if any), which can be achieved in a more cost-effective manner by better physical implementations and designs and better data independence support by commercial DBMSs

- May improve performance of some applications only at the expense of other applications

Furthermore, although dependency theory defines an end to the normalization process—tables in 3NF (or 5NF if keys are composite) [9]—the process of denormalization does not have a clear end [7]: Should tables be denormalized to 4NF, 3NF, 2NF, or 1NF? On what grounds? How much integrity risk and burden should users accept for unclear performance gains?

To the extent that current DBMS products leave no alternative, denormalization should be considered only as a last resort and *if and only if* "data items *(a)* are frequently retrieved together and *(b)* are rarely updated and *(c)* full normalization separates them in more than one table" [3]. But database designers should also understand all the implications of this approach, particularly for integrity, and document them. Such cases are, however, very rare in practice, and experience has shown that "basing database design on access patterns of known specific applications [biases] against others (including unforeseen ones) with different needs and that needs can also vary over time; the costs of denormalization end up outweighing performance benefits, if any; [contamination of] logical design with physical considerations [is something] users live to regret" [3].

A conclusion from Chapter 1 with respect to data types is equally applicable to normalization. To paraphrase, denormalization does not make redundancy and update anomalies or, for that matter, any other fundamental database issues and trade-offs go away; it simply ignores these issues. Users will be better off if they demand improvements from DBMS vendors, rather than undertake the burden—and risks—of working around product deficiencies.

References

[1]   C. J. Date, *An Introduction to Database Systems*, 6th ed., Reading, MA: Addison-Wesley, 1998.

[2]   C. J. Date, "Don't Mix Pointers and Relations," *Relational Database Writings 1994–1997*, Reading, MA: Addison-Wesley, 1998.

[3]   F. Pascal, *Understanding Relational Databases*, New York, NY: John Wiley & Sons, 1993.

[4]   C.J. Date, personal communication, 1999.

[5]   C. J. Date, "Functional Dependencies Are Fun," Parts 1–2, *Relational Database Writings 1994–1997*, Reading, MA: Addison-Wesley, 1998.

[6]   C. J. Date, "Normalization Is No Panacea," *Database Programming and Design*, April 1998.

[7]   C. J. Date, "The Normal Is So . . . Interesting," Parts 1–2, *Database Programming and Design*, November and December 1997.

[8] J. Reeder, "Denormalize at Your Own Risk," *InfoDB*, Fall 1989.

[9] C. J. Date, "The Final Normal Form!," Parts 1–2, *Database Programming and Design,* January and February 1998.

[10] C. J. Date, "What's Normal, Anyway?", *Database Programming and Design*, March 1998.

6

Neither Distinct nor the Same: Entity Supertypes and Subtypes

Let's start with three tables: CUSTOMERS, VENDORS, PHONES. All have a counter ID as primary key. There are one-to-many relationships between vendors and phones and between customers and phones. The foreign key in PHONES is the vendor/customer ID. I now have a problem, because a vendor and a customer may have the same key value. So I add a new column in PHONES called TYPE, which has values of 'V' or 'C.' The foreign key is now (ID,TYPE). Is this good design? Another solution is to have two phone tables. But one phone table is nice because in this particular environment, searching for the phone and finding who it belongs to is handy.

—ONLINE MESSAGE

6.1 The Issue

Two entities are of distinct types if they have no attributes in common. Logical relationships between entities of distinct types can be one-to-one (1:1), many-to-one (M:1), and many-to-many (M:M) (M:M relationships are represented by two M:1 relationships). Relationships are represented in the database by foreign key–primary key **referential integrity constraints**. It is, however, possible for entities to have *both* common and distinct attributes. If they have a *common identifier*, then they have a special referential relationship, an entity supertype-subtype relationship, which must also be identified during business modeling and mapped correctly to the logical model, such that redundancy and complications will not occur.

149

The SQL:99 standard (formerly known as SQL3) proposes "subtables" that "inherit" columns from "supertables," a feature that is neither well defined, nor the correct solution. SQL DBMSs do not support it anyway. This not only contributes to poor understanding of such relationships by users and induces poor database design, but also robs proper design from its practical benefits.

This chapter

- Explains the entity supertype-subtype relationship

- Provides design guidelines for the modeling of such relationships and demonstrates the usefulness of such designs

- Specifies what correct DBMS support should be

- Assesses the practical consequences of SQL's "approach"

- Offers practical recommendations

6.2 Fundamentals

The first step in database design is the development of a business model of the segment of reality of interest to be represented in the database. This is an *informal* endeavor based on subjective, selective *perceptions* of reality. The traditional approach is to identify entity types, attributes, and logical relationships of interest. In the second step, the business model is mapped to a **logical model** by means of a (preferably *formal*) **data model**. In the relational data model, time-varying named tables loosely represent entity types, columns represent attributes, and rows represent entities, desirably of only one type [1] (see Chapter 5). Tables can be viewed, therefore, as logical representations of the entity types that are identified in the real world during business modeling. Entity types are collections of the entities' attributes of interest. Without a *well-defined and complete* business model—entity types, attributes, and relationships—nothing can be said of the correctness of a logical design.

> ❖ **Note:** As reiterated throughout the book, *formally* tables represent *predicates*—generalized forms of propositions—columns represent value placeholders, and rows represent propositions. But *informally*, propositions can be viewed as assertions of fact *about entities*. Database practitioners are more familiar with the terminology of entities and attributes, which is fuzzy, but will suffice for the purposes of this discussion (but see the Note in section 6.2.2). The (informal) term "entity" subtype should not be confused with the (formal) term "data" type (or domain) discussed in Chapter 1, as the two are distinct.

6.2.1 Entity Types, Attributes, and Relationships

Entities in the real world are of one type if they have *all* their attributes—including the identifying attribute—in common. For example, all departments have department number (identifier), name, and budget as attributes, so they are entities of type Department, which maps logically to one table.

DEPARTMENTS {DEPT#,DNAME,BUDGET}

Similarly, all employees have an employee number (identifier), name, and hire date as attributes, so they are entities of a type Employee, which also maps logically to a table.

EMPLOYEES {EMP#,ENAME,HIREDATE}

Entities that have *no* attributes in common are of distinct types. Thus, the entity type Department is distinct from the entity type Employee. But what about entities with *both* common and distinct attributes?

Suppose that employees are assigned to departments, so department number is now an attribute shared with employees, but all other attributes remain distinct. This many-to-one relationship between employees and departments is represented in the database by the column DEPT# being a foreign key in EMPLOYEES, which references the primary key column in DEPARTMENTS.

```
EMPLOYEES {EMP#,ENAME,DEPT#,HIREDATE}
```

Departments and employees are still distinct entity types because they *do not share the identifier.* Departments are identified by DEPT#, employees by EMP#.

Suppose, now, that all employees are salaried, but some also earn commissions. Thus, in addition to the attributes common to all employees, some employees have commission as a distinct attribute. If all employees were considered entities of just one type, Employee would map to the table in Figure 6.1, where there are no COMMISSION values in rows representing salary-only employees because commission does not apply to them. But there is no such thing as "inapplicable

EMP#	ENAME	DEPT#	HIREDATE	SALARY	COMMISSION
100	Spenser	E21	06-19-1980	26150	
110	Lucchessi	A00	05-16-1958	38170	
120	O'Connell	A00	12-05-1963	37950	
130	Quintana	C01	07-28-1971	33800	
140	Nicholls	C01	12-15-1976	35420	
150	Adamson	D11	02-12-1972	30280	
160	Pianka	D11	10-11-1977	27250	
290	Parker	D31	05-30-1980	15340	4780
310	Setright	D31	09-12-1964	15900	3200

Figure 6.1. *Employees as Entities of One Type*

attributes" in the real world—those employees simply *do not possess* that attribute—so this design is not an accurate representation of reality and causes problems for database use (see Chapter 10).

On the other hand, viewing salaried and commissioned employees as entities of two entirely distinct types, say, Salaried-Employee and Commissioned-Employee, would lead to the two-table design in Figure 6.2. Although the inapplicable values were eliminated, there is now redundancy: The common information in the rows representing the two employees who earn both salary and commission repeats in both tables. Cross-table duplication of rows, or parts thereof, imposes its own set of problems (see Chapters 4 and 8).

EMP#	ENAME	DEPT#	HIREDATE	SALARY
100	Spenser	E21	06-19-1980	26150
110	Lucchessi	A00	05-16-1958	38170
120	O'Connell	A00	12-05-1963	37950
130	Quintana	C01	07-28-1971	33800
140	Nicholls	C01	12-15-1976	35420
150	Adamson	D11	02-12-1972	30280
160	Pianka	D11	10-11-1977	27250
290	Parker	D31	05-30-1980	15340
310	Setright	D31	09-12-1964	15900

SAT_EMP

EMP#	ENAME	DEPT#	HIREDATE	SALARY
290	Parker	D31	05-30-1980	4780
310	Setright	D31	09-12-1964	3200

COM_EMP

Figure 6.2. *Employees Viewed as Entities of Two Distinct Types*

It seems as if salaried and commissioned employees are neither entities of the same type, nor of completely distinct types.

6.2.2 A Special Case

By virtue of their common attributes—which *include the identifier*—all
employees are entities of type Employee. By virtue of their additional
distinct attribute, commission, the employees who also earn a commission are Commissioned-Employee entities, a **subtype** of the Employee
entity, an entity **supertype**. Subtype entities have the common
attributes of the supertype, *plus* their own distinct attributes. This is
another way of saying that every commissioned employee is an
employee, but not every employee is a commissioned employee.

To avoid inapplicable values and redundancy in the database, the set
of common attributes map logically to a base table (here EMP), and
the set of distinct attributes of every entity subtype map to a base
table each (here COM_EMP), shown in Figure 6.3. An **entity subtype-**

EMP#	ENAME	DEPT#	HIREDATE	SALARY
100	Spenser	E21	06-19-1980	26150
110	Lucchessi	A00	05-16-1958	38170
120	O'Connell	A00	12-05-1963	37950
130	Quintana	C01	07-28-1971	33800
140	Nicholls	C01	12-15-1976	35420
150	Adamson	D11	02-12-1972	30280
160	Pianka	D11	10-11-1977	27250
290	Parker	D31	05-30-1980	15340
310	Setright	D31	09-12-1964	15900

EMP

EMP#	COMMISSION
290	4780
310	3200

COM_EMP

Figure 6.3. *Base Table Representation of Entity Subtype-Supertype Relationship*

supertype relationship is represented in the database by a *zero-or-one-to-one* (0/1:1) referential constraint, a special case of the general (0/1:M) referential constraint. The common identifier (here, EMP#) is *both* primary key and foreign key in the subtype table (here, COM_EMP), referencing the primary key in the entity supertype table (here, EMP).

Entity supertype(s) and subtype(s) map to *views*. Figure 6.4 shows the supertype view EMPLOYEES defined over the whole table EMP and the subtype view COMMISSIONED, a natural join of COM_EMP with EMP on EMP#.

EMP#	ENAME	DEPT#	HIREDATE	SALARY
100	Spenser	E21	06-19-1980	26150
110	Lucchessi	A00	05-16-1958	38170
120	O'Connell	A00	12-05-1963	37950
130	Quintana	C01	07-28-1971	33800
140	Nicholls	C01	12-15-1976	35420
150	Adamson	D11	02-12-1972	30280
160	Pianka	D11	10-11-1977	27250
290	Parker	D31	05-30-1980	15340
310	Setright	D31	09-12-1964	15900

EMPLOYEES

EMP#	ENAME	DEPT#	HIREDATE	SALARY	COMMISSION
290	Parker	D31	05-30-1980	15340	4780
310	Setright	D31	09-12-1964	15900	3200

COMMISSIONED

Figure 6.4. *Entity Subtype and Supertype Views*

❖ **Note:** Observe the difficulty with informal, imprecise concepts, such as entity: It is less intuitive to view the base table rows in Figure 6.3 as representing entities in the sense in which the view rows in Figure 6.4 do. But the formal interpretation of rows representing propositions suffers from no such difficulties. There are two kinds of proposition in the example: about employees and about commissioned employees. Because some facts about commissioned employees are contained in the propositions about employees (the common facts), there is nothing to be gained (and much to lose; see Chapters 4 and 8) from repeating those facts more than once in the database. As Codd, the creator of the relational model, put it, "Saying something more than once does not make it more true." Hence the design that avoids redundancy.

Suppose, now, that some of the employees are salaried and some are commissioned, *but not both.* Thus, in addition to the attributes common to all employees (employee number, name, department, and hire date), some employees have the distinct attribute salary and some have commission. The arguments in the previous example can be extended to this case, which yields two entity subtypes of Employee: Salaried-Employee and Commissioned-Employee (the design of the base tables and views is left as an exercise for the reader).

Finally, what if *either or both* salary and commission were possible? It should be obvious that the same principles apply and the base tables would be those in Figure 6.5. Note, again, that the design is devoid of inapplicable values and cross-table duplication (the views are left as another exercise for the reader).

6.2.3 DBMS Support

Because entity subtype-supertype relationships are referential relationships, a DBMS supporting referential integrity would permit the

EMP#	ENAME	DEPT#	HIREDATE
100	Spenser	E21	06-19-1980
110	Lucchessi	A00	05-16-1958
120	O'Connell	A00	12-05-1963
130	Quintana	C01	07-28-1971
140	Nicholls	C01	12-15-1976
150	Adamson	D11	02-12-1972
160	Pianka	D11	10-11-1977
290	Parker	D31	05-30-1980
300	Smith	D31	06-19-1972
310	Setright	D31	09-12-1964

EMP

EMP#	SALARY
100	26150
110	38170
120	37950
130	33800
140	35420
150	30280
160	27250
290	15340
310	15900

SAL_EMP

EMP#	COMMISSION
300	17750
290	4780
310	3200

COM_EMP

Figure 6.5. *Base Table Representation of Subtype-Supertype Relationship*

declaration of the pertinent foreign keys and referential rules and enforce them accordingly (see Chapters 2, 3). It would be very convenient, however, if the DBMS were cognizant of such relationships and were able to generate the appropriate views on its own. With a truly relational DBMS, most of the information necessary for that purpose is already in the table definition statements, and only a minor addition would be required for such a capability. Using, for example, a hypothetical SQL syntax, the three following CREATE TABLE statements for the base tables in Figure 6.5 would simply contain SUPERTYPE and SUBTYPE clauses (in bold).

```
CREATE TABLE emp
  (emp# ... DOMAIN emp#,
   ename ...,
   dept# ...,
   hiredate ...,
   PRIMARY KEY emp#
   SUPERTYPE employees);

CREATE TABLE sal_emp
  (emp# ... DOMAIN emp#,
   salary ...,
   PRIMARY KEY emp#
   FOREIGN KEY emp#
   REFERENCES emp
   SUBTYPE salaried);

CREATE TABLE com_emp
  (emp# ... DOMAIN emp#,
   commission ...,
   PRIMARY KEY emp#
   FOREIGN KEY emp#
   REFERENCES emp
   SUBTYPE commissioned;
```

The DBMS could be designed to interpret the SUPERTYPE clause in the first statement as an instruction to define the view EMPLOYEES as a projection on all EMP columns. And because the subtype views are joined on the declared primary-foreign key columns (EMP#), the DBMS could interpret the SUBTYPE clauses as instructions to generate SALARIED and COMMISSIONED join views similar to those in Figure 6.5. The DBMS integrity enforcement mechanism would enforce the referential constraints underlying the relationships.

Note that the DBMS would also have to support *multitable view updates* and correctly propagate them through to the underlying base tables [3, 4]. In fact, a truly relational DBMS with complete and correct support of keys (see Chapter 3) and integrity, including constraint inheritance and multitable view updating (see Chapter 2), would have little problem supporting this type of relationship.

6.3 Practical Implications

6.3.1 Multikey References

It is practical for every table with multiple candidate keys to have one selected as primary key for referential purposes. Other tables would then always reference the primary key (see Chapter 3). Consider a company that records information about job applicants as follows:

```
APPLICANTS {APPL#,LNAME,FNAME,...}
APPL_JOBS {APPL#,JOB#,EMPLOYER,START_DATE,...}
```

There can be multiple jobs per applicant, and they are identified by the {APPL#,JOB#} composite key. Then, for applicants who become employees

```
EMPLOYEES {EMP#,JOB#,DEPT#,PHONE,APPL#,...}
SAL_HIST {EMP#,SALARY,DATE,...}
```

> We have the very same entity being not only identified, but also referenced by an EMP# value in one [table] (SAL_HIST) and by an APPL# in others (APPL_JOBS, EMPLOYEES) . . . Now, we could avoid the apparent need for two different identifiers for the same entity type . . . but why should the enterprise change its way of doing business, just because of a piece of relational dogma? [5]

But if "the way of doing business" is not practical, the company should consider changing it. Because both APPL# and EMP# are essentially surrogate keys (see Chapter 3) and because some applicants do become employees, there are complications and no benefit from using two different identifiers for applicants and for employees. The situation is one of different *roles*—applicant and employee—with some persons switching roles. And depending on *what attributes of interest are recorded for either role*, applicants and employees can be viewed as entity subtypes of, say, a Person entity supertype. As persons, applicants and employees have some common attributes (at least name), but employees also have distinct attributes (job number, department number, hiredate, salary). Assuming that applicants have more distinct attributes than just application number (e.g., application date), applicants and employees can be viewed as subtypes of the entity supertype Person, and the logical design would be as follows

```
PERSONS {ID,LNAME,FNAME,...,ROLE}
APPS {ID,...}
EMPS {ID,JOB#,DEPT#,PHONE,...}
```

APPLICANTS and EMPLOYEES join views can then be derived accordingly (left as an exercise for the reader). This design uses one primary key for referential purposes—ID—and still preserves the distinction between applicants and employees as subtypes.

6.3.2 SQL Subtables and Supertables

The SQL:99 standard supports a table definition feature, whereby tables can be defined as "subtables" of "supertables" with an UNDER clause and "inherit" columns from their respective "supertables" [6]. In the case described in Figure 6.4, for example:

```
CREATE TABLE emp
  (emp# ...,
   ename ...,
   dept# ...,
   hiredate ...,
   salary ...,
   PRIMARY KEY emp#);
```

```
CREATE TABLE commissioned
  (emp# ...,
   commission ...,
   UNDER emp
   PRIMARY KEY emp#);
```

The intent behind this feature is, essentially, to present users with what seem to be two tables, but allow the DBMS "under the covers" to store the common attributes only once, thus avoiding physical redundancy. How exactly this is implemented "under the covers" is left to DBMS vendors. Thus, instead of the two base tables in Figure 6.3 and the two views in Figure 6.4, the user will *see* the two tables in Figure 6.6, but the common columns in the COMMISSIONED table are "virtual"—they are not physically stored.

Note very carefully that the relationship between a SQL subtable and supertable is *not a regular foreign key–primary key relationship.* To paraphrase,

> Suppose that an existing [salaried employee becomes commissioned]. If we simply try to insert an appropriate row into [COMMISSIONED], the system will attempt to insert a corresponding row into [EMP] as well—an attempt that will presumably fail on some kind of uniqueness violation. Thus, it looks as if we will need an additional form of INSERT ("INSERT ONLY"?) that will let us insert a row into the subtable only. Conversely, suppose an existing [commissioned employee] becomes [salaried]. If we simply try to delete the appropriate row from [COMMISSIONED], the system will delete the corresponding row from [EMPLOYEES] as well—a side effect that will presumably not be desired. Thus, it looks as if we will need an additional form of DELETE ("DELETE ONLY"?) that will let us delete a row from the subtable only. [6]

Because the same result can be obtained via the view mechanism, without additional structure, integrity, and operations that complicate

EMP#	ENAME	DEPT#	HIREDATE	SALARY
100	Spenser	E21	06-19-1980	26150
110	Lucchessi	A00	05-16-1958	38170
120	O'Connell	A00	12-05-1963	37950
130	Quintana	C01	07-28-1971	33800
140	Nicholls	C01	12-15-1976	35420
150	Adamson	D11	02-12-1972	30280
160	Pianka	D11	10-11-1977	27250
290	Parker	D31	05-30-1980	15340
310	Setright	D31	09-12-1964	15900

EMPLOYEES

Virtual Columns

EMP#	ENAME	DEPT#	HIREDATE	SALARY	COMMISSION
290	Parker	D31	05-30-1980	15340	4780
310	Setright	D31	09-12-1964	15900	3200

COMMISSIONED

Figure 6.6. *SQL Supertable and Subtable with "Virtual" Columns*

the data language, this feature is highly questionable. For example, the two views in Figure 6.4, equivalent to the supertable and subtable in Figure 6.6, can be readily created in SQL from the underlying base tables in Figure 6.3 as follows:

```
CREATE VIEW employees
  AS SELECT emp#,ename,dept#,hiredate,salary
     FROM emp;

CREATE VIEW commissioned
  AS SELECT emp#,ename,dept#,hiredate,commission
     FROM emp,com_emp
     WHERE emp.emp# = com_emp.emp#;
```

Be that as it may, commercial SQL implementations do not currently support this feature anyway. Neither do they support fully and properly—if at all—keys and integrity, particularly constraint inheritance (see Chapter 3). Without such support, insert, update, and delete operations on the views cannot be guaranteed to be correctly promulgated to the underlying base tables, which is why multitable views are not usually updatable in DBMS products.

> ❖ **Note:** A database table is a *variable*—its value changes over time as new rows are inserted and old rows are updated or deleted. Inheritance applies to values, not to variables. Thus "to talk of 'supertables and subtables' is to talk of what might perhaps be called 'supervariables and subvariables' . . . . whatever that might mean! (How can two distinct variables possibly be such that one is a 'subvariable' of the other?) . . . This insight immediately suggests that . . . the idea seems a little suspect right away" [6].

6.4 Conclusion and Recommendations

Database design is a three-level—conceptual, logical, physical—iterative endeavor, requiring an intimate, thorough knowledge of the segment of reality to be represented in the database [1]. The human mind is capable of intuitive shortcuts (e.g., identifying entity types and mapping them to tables in one step), but such shortcuts may also lead to incomplete, incorrect, or confused business models. Such outcomes are likely because business modeling is based on selective, subjective perceptions of reality, which can be quite subtle. What is more, design flaws at a higher level of representation cannot be resolved at lower levels, so logical models can degenerate rapidly as the example at the beginning of this chapter demonstrates.

Proper identification of entity subtype and supertype relationships is based on the attributes of interest—common and unique—identified during business modeling. Incomplete or fuzzy attribute specifications will lead to poor logical designs and will thus result in inaccurate or incomplete information in the database, complex or wrongly formulated queries, or wrong answers to those queries.

Claims to the contrary notwithstanding, SQL's lack of correct support for entity supertype and subtype relationships is not a relational weakness. Although the relational model does not explicitly specify such support, it does not preclude it. Indeed, it is precisely because SQL *fails* to support completely and correctly crucial relational features—integrity, view updatability—that DBMSs based on it are robbed of the ability to relieve users from the drudgery and error-proneness of undertaking the view definitions themselves, and even then the views are not updatable.

Users should identify entity subtypes and supertypes during business modeling, map them correctly to base tables, and define the pertinent views. But because SQL DBMSs usually do not permit updates on multitable views, users will have no choice but to resort to stored procedures (or, worse, application code) to update the base tables directly, with loss of logical data independence. This can be a serious burden in complex transaction environments, which can become prohibitive and increase integrity risks considerably. But the problems will be much more severe in the absence of such discipline.

References

[1] F. Pascal, *Understanding Relational Databases*, New York, NY: John Wiley & Sons, 1993.

[2] C. J. Date and D. McGoveran, "A New Database Design Principle," *Relational Database Writings 1991–1994*, Reading, MA: Addison-Wesley, 1995.

[3] C. J. Date and D. McGoveran, "Updating Union, Intersection and Difference Views," *Relational Database Writings 1991–1994*, Reading, MA: Addison-Wesley, 1995.

[4] C. J. Date and D. McGoveran, "Updating Joins and Other Views," *Relational Database Writings 1991–1994*, Reading, MA: Addison-Wesley, 1995.

[5] C. J. Date, "The Primacy of Primary Keys: An Investigation," *Relational Database Writings 1991–1994*, Reading, MA: Addison-Wesley, 1995.

[6] C. J. Date and H. Darwen, "Subtables and Supertables," *Foundation for Object/Relational Databases: The Third Manifesto*, Reading, MA: Addison-Wesley, 1998.

7

Climbing Trees in SQL: Data Hierarchies

Can somebody help me with some advice on how to display records from a "tree" structure table in a specified order? The table has three fields [and] an unknown number of hierarchy levels . . .

CODE	TITLE	PARENT
100	Total	
110	Europe	100
210	America	100
120	UK	110
130	France	110
140	Germany	110
230	Canada	210
220	USA	210

Any idea . . . [of] a generic SQL SELECT [statement], if there is one . . . that applies recursive[ly] a level number to each record and somehow includes that as part of a larger SELECT statement, [to ultimately] produce a bottom-to-top display in order of countries?
—ONLINE MESSAGE

7.1 The Issue

Attempts by DBMS vendors to fill the hierarchy handling gap in SQL have ignored sound logic principles. Consequently, when dealing with data hierarchies (also referred to as tree structures), users of SQL DBMSs must contend, at best, with unintuitive, difficult to express

SQL statements and/or worse, application code. These workarounds are complex, limited, problematic, lack DBMS optimization, and are proprietary to boot. With large and complex hierarchies, they are prohibitively prone to error and slow.

This chapter

- Expounds data hierarchy fundamentals
- Provides design guidelines for representing tree structures
- Clarifies the correct approach to hierarchic manipulation
- Assesses workarounds offered by SQL DBMSs

7.2 Fundamentals

True hierarchies, for example, geographic and political (countries, states, cities), organizational (departments), and component assembly structures involve "parent-child" relationships, where children nodes are descendants of parent nodes. Such structures are referred to as "trees" because every node, except the "root" one (usually at the top, though), has exactly one immediate parent node. The tree underlying the example at the beginning of the chapter is shown in Figure 7.1.

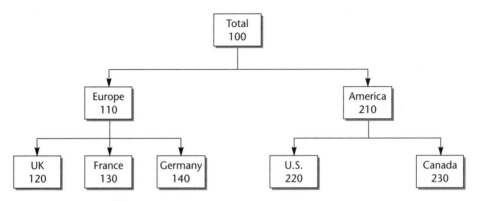

Figure 7.1. *True Hierarchy with Unique Nodes*

❖ **Note:** Structures where children have more than one immediate parent are **networks**; structures where nodes are—directly or indirectly—parents of themselves are **recursive**. While true hierarchies are perceived by some as self-recursive structures, for example, an organizational structure where the top department reports to itself and, thus, is its own parent, the tree analogy suggests that, like a root, the top node does not really have a parent. Networks and recursive structures are outside the scope of this discussion.

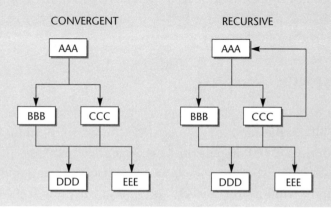

7.2.1 Nodes and Links

In the traditional entity-based approach to business modeling, each fully normalized table represents (loosely) an entity type (see Chapter 5). As indicated in the previous example, simple hierarchies are frequently represented by just one table. But such tables have at least one row—representing the root node—that is different from the others, an indication that not all entities represented by the table's rows are of only one type. Any design that "bundles" multiple entity types into one table produces complications and the need for special integrity constraints (see Chapters 3, 5, and 8), but in the case of tree structures, such lumping also causes "numerous database traversal problems" [1]. These complications can be avoided by separating the entity types into multiple tables.

There are, in fact, two types of entities in tree structures—nodes and links. The tree represented by the table in Figure 7.1 is a special simple case: The same geographic entity cannot occur more than once in the tree. Because all nodes are unique, the relationship between child and parent nodes is one-to-one. Consequently, the tree maps straightforwardly to two tables, NODES and LINKS, shown in Figure 7.2. CODE is the key in CODES, CCODE (child CODE) is the key in LINKS, and CCODE and PCODE (parent CODE) are foreign keys in LINKS, referencing CODE in NODES.

7.2.2 "Explode" Queries

A common type of query for databases representing tree structures is, "What are all the descendants of node X?" known in manufacturing as "bill-of-materials (BOM) explosions" because they "explode" (flatten) tree sections under specific nodes. In the previous example, the user wants to know what all the descendants are, direct and indirect, of the

CODE	NAME
100	TOTAL
110	EUROPE
210	AMERICA
140	GERMANY
130	FRANCE
120	UK
230	CANADA
220	US

NODES

CCODE	PCODE
220	210
120	110
110	100
210	100
130	110
140	110
230	210

LINKS

Figure 7.2. *Logical Database Representation of Hierarchy*

root node (X=100). The explosion is shown in Figure 7.3 where column CCODE contains all the descendants of the root node and PCODE contains the parent node to which the explosion applies (here, 100). Although the constant PCODE value may seem odd at this point, it will shortly prove to be essential.

7.2.3 Recurring Nodes

Consider now the part assembly in Figure 7.4 with multiple occurrences of the same part (P3, P6), some at *the same tree level*. Here nodes are not unique and, hence, there is a many-to-one (M:1) relationship between parts and nodes. The relationship between children and parents is many-to-many (M:M): The same part can have different immediate parents at different tree locations, and each parent can have different children either at different locations, or even at the same location. For example, part P3 on the second level has P1 as parent; on the third level it has P2 and P4 as parents; and part P6 on the third level has P3 and P4 as parents.

The NODES and LINKS tables representing this hierarchy are shown in Figure 7.5. P# and (CP#,PP#) are, respectively, the keys in NODES and LINKS; CP# and PP# are foreign keys in LINKS referencing P# (node

CCODE	PCODE
110	100
210	100
120	100
130	100
140	100
220	100
230	100

Figure 7.3. *Tree Explosion for the Root Node*

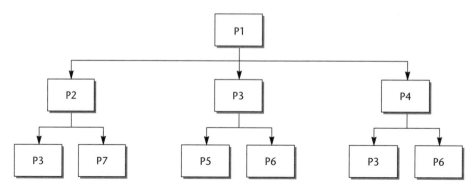

Figure 7.4. *Part Assembly Hierarchy*

attributes other than the identifier, e.g., part description, quantity, price, and so on, normally occurring in real-world part assemblies, are ignored for simplicity).

If the preceding explode operation were applied to the LINKS table, the result would contain duplicates, as shown in Figure 7.6 (it would lack a key). Now, because they are an incorrect representation of reality, the complications caused by duplicates should not occur in a relational

P#
P1
P2
P3
P4
P5
P6
P7

NODES

CP#	PP#
P2	P1
P3	P1
P4	P1
P3	P2
P7	P2
P5	P3
P6	P3
P3	P4
P6	P4

LINKS

Figure 7.5. *Database Representation of Part Assembly*

database (see Chapter 4), so an RDBMS would eliminate them from the result. This would cause information loss: It would not be possible to know from the result of the explode query that parts P3 and P6 are, directly and indirectly, children of part P1 more than once. This is offered as evidence that not only are duplicates benign, but they are actually essential in such cases.

But rows represent propositions asserted to be true (facts), so what do duplicates *mean*? This depends, of course, on what the informational intent of the database is. If propositions are about *parts*, regardless of how many times they occur in the tree, then the three duplicates {P3,P1} represent the proposition

Part **P3** *is descendant of part* **P1**

repeated three times, and the two duplicates {P6,P1} represent the proposition

Part **P6** *is descendant of part* **P1**

repeated twice. Asserting the same fact more than once has no informational value, which is why an RDBMS would remove duplicates (see Chapter 4).

CP#	PP#
P2	P1
P3	P1
P7	P1
P3	P1
P5	P1
P6	P1
P4	P1
P3	P1
P6	P1

Figure 7.6. *Explosion Result with Duplicates for Root Part*

If, on the other hand, the propositions are about *occurrences* of parts, then they should *identify* those occurrences. Part occurrences are identified by their tree *location*, but because the same part can occur more than once at the same tree level, the part name and level alone are not sufficient to uniquely identify occurrences. In the absence of a natural identifier, a surrogate key (see Chapter 3) will do, say, LINK, "a sequential number obtained by numbering the links (arcs in the tree) in depth-first (top-to-bottom, left-to-right) sequence, beginning with one" [2]. The propositions about part occurrences would be, therefore, different than those about parts. For the three occurrences of part P3 they would be

> *For link **2** part **P3** is descendant of part **P1** at level **3***
>
> *For link **4** part **P3** is descendant of part **P1** at level **2***
>
> *For link **8** part **P3** is descendant of part **P1** at level **3***

And for the two occurrences of part P6

> *For link **6** part **P6** is descendant of part **P1** at level **3***
>
> *For link **9** part **P6** is descendant of part **P1** at level **3***

The representation in the explosion result is shown in Figure 7.7.

Note, however, that although the assembly tree in Figure 7.4 can be constructed from the NODES and LINKS base tables in Figure 7.5, it *cannot* be from the explosion in Figure 7.7 because the explosion does not capture in its result all the information about the tree structure represented in the base tables. Capturing the complete information would come in handy because the exploded result could serve as a more convenient target for further querying than the original base tables could (which would be much more complex in the real world), and any structural information that is not captured will not be accessible to subsequent queries.

For a full capture, explosions must be performed *for every parent node* in the tree (here, P1, P2, P3, P4) and the results merged into a "grand

LINK	CP#	PP#	LEVEL
1	P2	P1	2
2	P3	P1	3
3	P7	P1	3
4	P3	P1	2
5	P5	P1	3
6	P6	P1	3
7	P4	P1	2
8	P3	P1	3
9	P6	P1	3

Figure 7.7. *Explosion Result for Root Node: Part Occurrences*

explosion" table, shown in Figure 7.8. The dotted lines separate the component explosions for clarity: The first nine rows are from the root node explosion in Figure 7.7, and the other sections are explosions for parent nodes P2, P3, and P4, respectively. The (composite) key is the combination of all columns.

The importance of the PCODE column in Figure 7.3 should now be clear: Like PCODE, PP# is required for unique row identification in grand explosion tables because LINK values are calculated *separately for each component* explosion and, therefore, without PP#, the result would contain duplicates.

A grand explosion, then, "flushes out" the distinction between multiple occurrences of the same part and represents it explicitly as values in tables, rather than implicitly in the order of duplicates. It is this flushing out of structural information that makes explosion results useful as targets for further querying about the structure. For example, the reader can verify that queries, such as "What descendants occur more than once at

LINK	CP#	PP#	LEVEL
1	P2	P1	2
2	P3	P1	3
3	P7	P1	3
4	P3	P1	2
5	P5	P1	3
6	P6	P1	3
7	P4	P1	2
8	P3	P1	3
9	P6	P1	3
1	P3	P2	3
2	P7	P2	3
1	P5	P3	3
2	P6	P3	3
1	P3	P4	3
2	P6	P4	3

Figure 7.8. *Grand Explosion of the Part Assembly*

the second level?" are easier to express against the grand explosion result in Figure 7.8, than against the original base tables in Figure 7.5.

Proponents of duplicates claim that while generating columns such as LINK and LEVEL may be possible for relatively simple trees, doing so is difficult for real-world, large, and complex hierarchies. For example, if multiple occurrences of the same part on the same tree level have, as in Figure 7.9, the *same parent* (both occurrences of P5 and P6 have P3 as parent on the fourth level), then LINK and LEVEL are no longer suf-

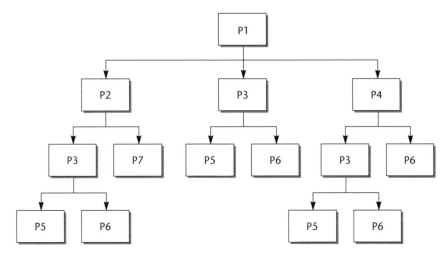

Figure 7.9. *Another Part Assembly*

ficient for unique identification and an additional surrogate key would have to be generated. For more complex structures "we could not even say how many extra columns would be needed to distinguish the duplicates by retaining their origins" [3].

But it is precisely when hierarchies are large and complex, though, that duplicates wreak havoc with the interpretability of query results (see Chapter 4). And unique identification would not be difficult if the DBMS were "more helpful and provide[d] a 'keying' function to generate unique identifiers systematically" [4]. In conjunction with such a function, an RDBMS could support a relational explosion operation, which, when applied to base tables such as LINKS, representing hierarchies of arbitrary complexity, would produce grand explosions by

1. Propagating explosion tables for all parent nodes, generating identifiers as necessary and uniquely naming their columns

2. Applying the union operation to the explosion tables in Step 1, inferring the key of the result in the process (see Chapter 2)

> ❖ **Note:** Although all the theoretical issues for a general DBMS keying capability have not yet been resolved, general guidelines for a systematic function have been formally proposed [5].

One of the most important practical benefits from relational theory is that table operations can be *nested* arbitrarily to any depth, either explicitly by users, or by the DBMS (which can also exploit nestability for performance optimization purposes) [6, 7]. Thus, any relational operations (project, restrict, and so on) could be nested with a relational explosion operation to answer queries about the tree structure. Once users provide the hierarchic information in LINKS-type base tables during database design, such explosion operations could be applied to generate snapshot tables, which could then serve as input for all queries about the hierarchy. Snapshot tables do not pose redundancy problems because they are query-only and need to be refreshed only if and when the tree structure changes [6].

7.3 Practical Implications

7.3.1 SQL and Trees

The SQL standard has not, as of this writing, included functionality for the processing of data hierarchies (but see the guidelines below). There is, therefore, no single SQL statement that explodes single-node or full tree structures. Because it fails to adhere to relational (as well as proper language design) principles [6], SQL requires major surgery to produce results equivalent to those of a relational explosion.

Guidelines for a recursive EXPLODE() table function were suggested early on [2], as follows:

```
SELECT columnlist
FROM EXPLODE(x)
WHERE (restrict conditions)
```

where X is a table such as LINKS. Such statements would produce the single-node explosions and simultaneously query them (via projection on the SELECT-list, restrictions with WHERE clauses and, possibly further nesting with other operations), but they would have to be explicitly UNIONed by users into grand explosions.

Some DBMS products implement proprietary extensions to SQL for processing data hierarchies. But because they too ignore relational principles (to avoid major surgery), these features are limited, cumbersome, unintuitive, procedural, and problematic. One product, for example, implemented a proprietary CONNECT BY clause in its SQL dialect. The result in Figure 7.3 can be obtained by running the following query against the LINKS table in Figure 7.2

```
SELECT ccode,100 AS pcode
FROM links
CONNECT BY PRIOR ccode=pcode
START with ccode=100
```

The problem is that if a similar query were run against the LINKS table in Figure 7.5, namely

```
SELECT ccode,'P1' AS pcode
FROM links
CONNECT BY PRIOR ccode=pcode
START with ccode='P1'
```

it would yield the result with duplicates in Figure 7.6, with all the negative implications already discussed.

❖ **Note:** Criticism of the CONNECT BY clause is frequently dismissed; for example, *"The result of a SQL [CONNECT BY] statement . . . is a table [to which] another SQL statement [can be applied] . . . The [proprietary] clause does have restrictions on its use with subqueries and joins, but . . . it does generate a table and, thus, satisfies the definition of closure"* [7]. In other words, a table is a table is a table, so what's the fuss?

But, first, nestability of subqueries and joins is exactly what is desirable for manipulation of CONNECT BY results, and restricting it severely limits the clause's usefulness. Second, as already explained "If . . . [such results] are fed as input to another operation, then the information represented by the [duplicates and] ordering of the rows will simply be lost" [7, 8]. Indeed, the UNION operation to which the results of CONNECT BY queries would be input for the generation of grand explosions *eliminates duplicates*; with other operations, the DBMS may reorder the table, if desirable for optimization purposes. These are the exact reasons for which SQL limits nestability.

A proper relational explode operation that makes explicit the information embedded in the duplicates and row order yields results that lose no information during further manipulation. Can CONNECT BY be used to produce equivalent results? It is possible to write a SQL statement with this clause for each parent node in the hierarchy in Figure 7.4, projecting on PCODE and relying on two of the product's system-generated *implicit* columns, ROWNUM (for LINK) and LEVEL. But this approach

- Requires user awareness of the existence of implicit system columns (one of which, ROWNUM, was never intended for this use and exists only for base tables, precluding explosions on derived tables)

- Suffers from restrictions that CONNECT BY imposes on SQL statements

- Requires the explicit UNIONing of single-node CONNECT BY SQL statements

- Because it is somewhat procedural, it does not benefit from DBMS optimization

- Is proprietary

What is more, even this cumbersome approach breaks down with trees like the one in Figure 7.9 because the DBMS cannot produce identifiers beyond the two system columns.

An even more "manual" approach, implemented by another product, is being incorporated into the SQL standard [8]. The explosion for the root node of the tree in Figure 7.4 would be expressed as

```
WITH parent (cp#,pp#)
AS (SELECT cp#,pp#
    FROM links
    WHERE pp#='P1'
    UNION ALL
    SELECT l.cp#,l.pp#
    FROM links l,parent p
    WHERE l.pp# = p.cp#)
SELECT cp#,'P1'
FROM parent;
```

which, when applied to the LINKS table in Figure 7.5, would yield the result in Figure 7.6, with duplicates and a *different numbering order*, left-to-right, top-to-bottom. Note, first, that this is also a procedural, stepwise operation, including the explicit use of a temporary table (PARENT) and a separate SELECT statement to project and/or restrict toward the desired result (unlike a relational solution, such as EXPLODE(), where the result could be projected and restricted within the same statement). Second, the operation uses the nonrelational version of the UNION operator, UNION ALL, to preserve the duplicates in the result, which would also have to be used to merge such results into a grand explosion and which inhibits optimization (see Chapter 4). There seems to be a way to generate a column like LEVEL in Figure 7.7 by using a form of explicit looping

```
WITH parent (cp#,pp#,level)
AS (SELECT DISTINCT cp#,pp#,0
    FROM links
    WHERE pp#='P1'
    UNION ALL
    SELECT l.cp#,l.pp#,l.level +1
    FROM links l,parent p
    WHERE l.pp# = p.cp#)
SELECT cp#,'P1',level
FROM parent;
```

But there seems to be no DBMS capability for generating more identifiers or handling more complex trees like that in Figure 7.9. The feature seems "hamstrung by having to be part of SQL! . . . there is an extreme lack of orthogonality—no DISTINCT with UNION ALL (which retains duplicates), no GROUP BY, no HAVING, no subqueries, etc." [10]. The operation seems to have no formal definition and, thus, has questionable reliability and generalizability. And it is certainly *not* intuitive or "convenient" to express.

7.4 Conclusion and Recommendations

Relational handling of tree structures in databases would be more intuitive and convenient to express, would be nonprocedural, and would not be handicapped by duplicates. The DBMS would execute all the steps transparently, would optimize performance, and in conjunction with a key generation facility (see Chapter 3), would work with any true hierarchy. But because it is difficult to implement post hoc in systems with a weak relational foundation, SQL and its commercial dialects do not support such functionality. Faced with the workarounds, users blame the purportedly relational nature of SQL for the deficiencies.

> *My company could not care less if I know [relational] terms—they want the results . . . we have to work with what we have, not what we wish it were. So products are not "truly" relational. My questions would be along the lines of "How can I get it to do X?" Do I really care what the terms are in relation to [products]? No!*
> —TRADE PUBLICATION ARTICLE

Actually, just the opposite is true: It is *failure* to adhere to relational principles (as well as to principles of good language design) that makes tree processing difficult in SQL. But if users *don't even know what they "wish it were,"* how will they ever get it in products? Without user pressure on DBMS vendors to provide the right solutions, none will materialize and users will continue to ask "How can I get it to do X?"—which, as this chapter demonstrates, is *less*, not more practical. Worse, users are unaware that they erroneously blame the problems on the very technology that can resolve them. The only recommendation is for users to educate themselves on and demand the correct solution from DBMS vendors.

References

[1] Interview with David McGoveran, *Database Newsletter*, July/August 1996.

[2] C. J. Date, "A Note on the Part Explosion Problem," *Relational Database Selected Writings*, Reading, MA: Addison-Wesley, 1986.

[3] H. Darwen, "The Duplicity of Duplicate Rows," *Rational Database Writings 1989–1991*, Reading, MA: Addison-Wesley, 1992.

[4] C. J. Date and H. Darwen, *Foundation for Object/Relational Databases: The Third Manifesto*, Reading, MA: Addison-Wesley, 1998.

[5] F. Pascal, *Understanding Relational Databases, New York, NY: John Wiley & Sons, 1993.*

[6] C. J. Date, "The Importance of Closure," *Relational Database Writings 1991–1994*, Reading, MA: Addison-Wesley, 1993.

[7] C. J. Date, Appendix, *Database Programming and Design*, May 1993.

[8] G. E. Birchall, *DB2/V2 SQL Cookbook*, January 1996.

[9] C. J. Date, personal communication, 1999.

8

Not Worth Repeating: Redundancy

Say you have a table CUST[OMER] with fields ID [and] DEBT, showing how much each customer owed before any payments and a PAYMENT table with fields ID (nonunique) [and] PYMT . . . the amount of each payment. I find myself forced for the second time . . . [to add and maintain] redundant fields [—SUMPAY in CUST[OMER]—] because SQL is too slow . . . so I have to remember whenever [updating] payments to make the corresponding change in CUST[OMER]. To find paid-up customers you'd have to (as far as I know) do it in two steps (following is pseudocode):

```
SELECT c.id, c.debt, SUM(p.pymt) AS sumpay
FROM customer c, payments p
WHERE c.id = p.id
INTO temptable

SELECT id
FROM temptable
WHERE debt <= sumpay
```

(Or is there a one-step solution?) I was wondering if [standard] SQL has provision[s] for storing and maintaining [automatically] redundant info[rmation]. Wouldn't this be desirable?

—ONLINE MESSAGE

8.1 The Issue

Minimizing—if not eliminating—redundancy is a major objective in database management and, indeed, one of the main reasons for the move from application-specific data files to centralized databases [1]. Aside from waste of storage space at the physical level, redundancy increases the potential for inconsistency and imposes additional integrity burdens at the logical level on both users and the DBMS. Space inefficiency translates to costly time inefficiency when doing backup, restore, recovery, load, export, index creation, and so on. Thus, except for certain specialized contexts where such complications do not arise (e.g., historical data, recovery logs), or where certain minor inconsistencies can be consciously tolerated (e.g., decision support), redundancy imposes heavy costs but offers no benefit.

This chapter

- Documents the various kinds of database redundancy
- Explains their origins and consequences
- Provides design guidelines for avoiding or removing redundancy
- Clarifies integrity requirements for redundancy control by the DBMS
- Concludes with some practical recommendations

8.2 Fundamentals

A database table represents a time-varying set of propositions about entities (desirably of one type; see Chapter 5). Propositions are assertions of fact about entities of interest or, loosely, sets of attribute values of those entities. Because entities are distinct in the real world, each proposition must include a value for its entity's *identifying* attribute, which distinguishes it from all other entities and propositions. All other attribute values in a proposition are about the entity identified by that identifying attribute or, in short, about the identifier (see Chapter 5). Propositions are represented by rows and attributes by columns; the identifier is represented by one or more key column(s). Redundancy occurs if and when whole propositions, or parts thereof, are recorded more than once in the database. Redundancy increases the potential for inconsistency.

> [If] a given fact about the real world . . . is represented by two distinct entries in the stored database . . . [and] the DBMS is not

aware of this duplication (i.e., the redundancy is not *controlled*), [t]hen there will necessarily be occasions on which the two entries will not agree—namely, when one of the two has been updated and the other has not. At such times, the database is said to be inconsistent. Clearly, a database that is in an inconsistent state is capable of supplying incorrect or contradictory information to its users. It should also be clear that if the given fact is represented by a single entry (i.e., if the redundancy is removed), then such an inconsistency cannot occur. [2]

In other words, redundancy control imposes additional integrity burdens on users and the DBMS, which would otherwise be unnecessary. Unless redundancy is avoided by design, or eliminated by redesign (see Chapter 5), additional integrity constraints need to be declared by users and enforced by the DBMS or, if the DBMS does not enforce them, by users via application code.

There are several types of redundancy.

8.2.1 Duplicate Rows

Because in the real world distinct entities are by definition uniquely identifiable—that is how we know they are distinct—for a database representation to be accurate, each table must have at least one key (see Chapter 3) representing the identifying attribute(s). Consequently, duplicate rows—be they *within* tables (see Chapter 4) or *across* tables (see Section 8.2.1.2)—are one form of redundancy due to inaccurate representation of reality.

8.2.1.1 Within-Table Duplicates

A supermarket, for example, could represent cake mix boxes as duplicate rows in its inventory database, as shown in Figure 8.1. Such

DESCRIPTION	PRICE
Cake mix box	1.10
Cake mix box	1.10

Figure 8.1. *Duplicate Rows*

tables do not have a key. As incomplete representations, duplicates lead to difficult to interpret and misleading query results and inhibit query expression transformations for performance optimization purposes (see Chapter 4).

Duplicate rows should, therefore, be avoided (rather than allowed in the database and then sought out and removed) by defining a key for every base table, even if a surrogate key, as in Figure 8.2 (see Chapter 3).

> ❖ **Note:** If the DBMS supports keys fully and correctly, including **key inheritance**, it can infer the keys of derived tables, such as views, from the keys of the underlying base tables and the table operation used to derive the views (see Chapters 2 and 3).

8.2.1.2 Cross-Table Duplicates

Suppose that employees had several common attributes of interest (name, department, hire date), but some were salaried, others commis-

ITEM#	DESCRIPTION	PRICE
1	Cake mix box	1.10
2	Cake mix box	1.10

Figure 8.2. *Duplicate Rows*

sioned, and some earned both a salary and a commission. One possible conceptualization is of two distinct entity types, Salaried-Employee and Commissioned-Employee, mapping to the two tables in Figure 8.3. Note that information about employees who earn both a salary and a commission (highlighted) is recorded in both tables.

Like their within-table counterparts, cross-table duplicates are a type of redundancy due to incorrect representation of reality. This is indicated by a logical contradiction: The two tables supposedly represent *distinct* entity types, but no unique attribute is represented that makes them distinct. In addition to update anomalies, cross-table duplication

EMP#	ENAME	DEPT#	HIREDATE	SALARY	COMMISSION
100	Spenser	E21	06-19-1980	26150	
110	Lucchessi	A00	05-16-1958	38170	
120	O'Connell	A00	12-05-1963	37950	
130	Quintana	C01	07-28-1971	33800	
140	Nicholls	C01	12-15-1976	35420	
150	Adamson	D11	02-12-1972	30280	
160	Pianka	D11	10-11-1977	27250	
290	Parker	D31	05-30-1980	15340	4780
310	Setright	D31	09-12-1964	15900	3200

SAL_EMP

EMP#	ENAME	DEPT#	HIREDATE	SALARY	COMMISSION
290	Parker	D31	05-30-1980	15340	4780
310	Setright	D31	09-12-1964	15900	3200
300	Smith	D31	06-19-1972	17750	

COM_EMP

Figure 8.3. *Employees Viewed as Entities of Two Distinct Types*

of rows, or parts thereof (see next section), cause problems for view updating [3] (see Chapter 2). To avoid these complications, the **principle of orthogonal design** prohibits full or partial cross-table duplication in the database [4]. Such redundancy should either be avoided by design or removed by redesign, as shown in the next sections.

8.2.2 Entity Subtypes and Supertypes

An alternative design to that in Figure 8.3 is shown in Figure 8.4. It avoids inapplicable values and cross-table duplicates, but note that

EMP#	ENAME	DEPT#	HIREDATE	SALARY
100	Spenser	E21	06-19-1980	26150
110	Lucchessi	A00	05-16-1958	38170
120	O'Connell	A00	12-05-1963	37950
130	Quintana	C01	07-28-1971	33800
140	Nicholls	C01	12-15-1976	35420
150	Adamson	D11	02-12-1972	30280
160	Pianka	D11	10-11-1977	27250
290	Parker	D31	05-30-1980	15340
310	Setright	D31	09-12-1964	15900

SAL_EMP

EMP#	ENAME	DEPT#	HIREDATE	COMMISSION
300	Smith	D31	06-19-1972	17750
290	Parker	D31	05-30-1980	4780
310	Setright	D31	09-12-1964	3200

COM_EMP

Figure 8.4. *Entities with Common and Unique Attributes*

some redundancy remains: The *common* information for the two employees who are both salaried and commissioned is repeated in both tables. Asserting parts of a fact more than once has the same consequences as repeating the whole fact.

If entities have both common attributes, *including the identifying attribute*, as well as distinct attributes, they form an entity subtype-supertype relationship. In this example, salaried employees and commissioned employees are subtypes of employee—the supertype. The subtypes have the common attributes of the supertype plus the distinct attributes of their own (here, salary and/or commission). A three-table design as in Figure 8.5 avoids redundancy. The entity subtypes and supertype map to views (see Chapter 6).

8.2.3 Column Dependencies

If tables were designed such that their rows represented propositions about entities of only one type, that is, if they were *fully* normalized, then all nonkey columns in a table would represent attributes of entities of that type. Entities are identified in the database by key values, so *all* nonkey columns in a fully normalized table would be dependent on the key or would be "about the key" (see Chapter 5). Because key values are unique and do not repeat, the values of the columns dependent on the key will not repeat either. Without redundancy, there is no risk of inconsistency and, consequently, the key constraint (uniqueness) is sufficient to ensure table integrity (see Chapter 2). Conversely, nonkey columns that are dependent on other nonkey columns (which means more than one entity type is represented) can have values that repeat. Much, *though not all*, database redundancy is due to such column dependencies. Unless the tables are normalized further, additional constraints to *control* the redundancy must be declared and enforced (see Chapter 3).

EMP#	ENAME	DEPT#	HIREDATE
100	Spenser	E21	06-19-1980
110	Lucchessi	A00	05-16-1958
120	O'Connell	A00	12-05-1963
130	Quintana	C01	07-28-1971
140	Nicholls	C01	12-15-1976
150	Adamson	D11	02-12-1972
160	Pianka	D11	10-11-1977
290	Parker	D31	05-30-1980
300	Smith	D31	06-19-1972
310	Setright	D31	09-12-1964

EMP

EMP#	SALARY
100	26150
110	38170
120	37950
130	33800
140	35420
150	30280
160	27250
290	15340
310	15900

SAL_EMP

EMP#	COMMISSION
300	17750
290	4780
310	3200

COM_EMP

Figure 8.5. *Entity Subtype-Supertype Base Table Representation*

❖ **Note:** Because they represent one entity type, fully normalized tables are also easier to understand and work with; if tables bundle entity types, it is less clear where certain information resides, and expressing certain queries can be less straightforward.

8.2.3.1 Functional Dependencies

Dependency on Part of the Key. The table ASSIGNS in Figure 8.6 records information about project managers, manager departments,

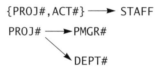

PROJ#	ACT#	PMGR#	DEPT#	STAFF
AD3111	20	20	A00	0.80
AD3111	30	20	A00	1.50
AD3111	40	20	A00	1.00
AD3111	50	20	A00	1.25
AD3111	60	20	A00	0.75
AD3111	70	20	A00	0.35
MA2100	20	10	D11	0.50
MA2100	30	10	D11	1.00
OP1000	30	10	D11	0.25
IF1000	30	20	A00	1.00
IF1000	50	20	A00	0.50
IF1000	60	20	A00	0.50

ASSIGNS

Figure 8.6. *Functional Dependency*

and staffing of project activities, and the key {PROJ#,ACT#} is composite. Although STAFF is functionally dependent on the key, PMGR# and DEPT# are functionally dependent on PROJ#, which is only one component of the key, not the whole key (formally, the table is not in second normal form, or 2NF).

As only part of the key, PROJ#'s values are not guaranteed to be unique. The values of the two dependent columns PMGR# and DEPT# repeat in every row with the same PROJ# value, causing the redundancy highlighted in Figure 8.6. This redundancy (and the accompanying update anomalies and potential inconsistencies) can be avoided by design or eliminated by further normalization via decomposition into two projections, each representing one of the entity types (see Chapter 5).

```
ACTSTAFF {PROJ#,ACT#,STAFF}
PROJASGN {PROJ#,PMGR#,DEPT#}
```

Otherwise, an integrity constraint must be explicitly declared and enforced in addition to the key constraint (see Section 8.3.3) to control the redundancy and ensure consistency.

Indirect Dependency. Figure 8.7 shows the PROJASGN projection from the previous example. Only PMGR# is directly dependent on the key. DEPT# is only *transitively* (indirectly) functionally dependent on PROJ# via the latter's dependency on PMGR# (formally, the table is not in third normal form, or 3NF).

```
PROJ# → PMGR# → DEPT#
```

Obviously, some redundancy remains: DEPT# values repeat with repeating PROJ# values, as highlighted in Figure 8.7. This redundancy (and the accompanying update anomalies and potential inconsistency) can be avoided by design or eliminated by further normalization via decomposition of the table into two 3NF projections, each representing one entity type (see Chapter 5).

```
PROJMGR {PROJ#,PMGR#}
PROJDPT {PMGR#,DEPT#}
```

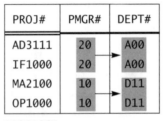

PROJASGN

Figure 8.7. *Transitive Functional Dependency*

Otherwise, an integrity constraint must be explicitly declared and enforced in addition to the key constraint (see Section 8.3.3) to control the redundancy and ensure consistency.

> ❖ **Note:** 3NF tables with multiple simple candidate keys are devoid of redundancy caused by column dependencies and, thus, are fully normalized. 3NF tables with *composite* keys can still suffer from redundancy and require further normalization. A normal form stronger than 3NF—Boyce-Codd normal form (BCNF)—generalizes 3NF to cover tables with multiple composite keys that *overlap* (see Chapter 3), which, if not in BCNF, require an explicit redundancy-controlling constraint [2].

8.2.4 Multivalued Dependencies

The table ASSIGNS in Figure 8.8 represents employee assignments to projects and activities and has the composite key {EMP#,PROJECT,ACTIV-ITY}. Given the business rule that these assignments are independent of one another, an employee can be assigned to project P1 and activity A even if activity A is not an activity of project P1, but of P2.

EMP#	PROJ	ACT
130	Query Services	DEBUG
130	Query Services	SUPP
130	User Education	DEBUG
130	User Education	SUPP
30	Query Services	DEBUG
30	Query Services	TEST
30	Query Services	CODE

ASSIGNS

Figure 8.8. *Multivalued Dependency*

There are *intra-key* dependencies: The PROJ and ACT key columns are *multivalued dependent* on EMP#, another key column (formally, the table is not in fourth normal form, or 4NF).

Sets of values of the dependent columns PROJ and ACT repeat with repeating EMP# values, causing the redundancy highlighted in Figure 8.8. This redundancy (and accompanying update anomalies and potential inconsistency) can be avoided by design or eliminated by further normalization via decomposition into two 4NF projections, each representing one type of assignment (see Chapter 5).

```
PROJASGN {EMP#,PROJ}
ACTASGN {EMP#,ACT}
```

Otherwise, an integrity constraint must be explicitly declared to and enforced by the DBMS in addition to the key constraint (see Section 8.3.3) to control the redundancy and ensure consistency.

8.2.5 Join Dependencies

The table in Figure 8.9 also represents assignments of employees to projects and activities. However, now project assignments and activity assignments are *not* independent (the business rule is: if an employee works for project P and project P has activity A and the employee is assigned to activity A, then the employee works for project P and is assigned to activity A). Here there are three intra-key **join dependencies** (formally, the table is not in fifth normal form, or 5NF).

This design produces redundancies of the type highlighted in Figure 8.9. Such redundancy (and accompanying update anomalies and potential inconsistency) can be avoided by design or eliminated by

{EMP#,PROJ,ACT} **JD** {EMP#,PROJ}
{EMP#,PROJ,ACT} **JD** {PROJ,ACT}
{EMP#,PROJ,ACT} **JD** {EMP#,ACT}

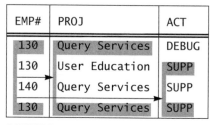

ASSIGNS

Figure 8.9. *Join Dependency*

further normalization via decomposition of the table into *three* 5NF projections, each representing one entity type (see Chapter 5).

PROJASGN {EMP#,PROJ}
ACTASGN {EMP#,ACT}
PROJACT {PROJ,ACT}

Otherwise, an integrity constraint must be explicitly declared to and enforced by the DBMS in addition to the key constraint (see Section 8.3.3) to control the redundancy and ensure consistency.

8.2.6 Derived Information

Consider the tables

CUSTOMERS {CUST#,DEPT,PAID}
PAYMENTS {CUST#,PDATE,PAYAMT}

where PAID is the total amount paid to date by each customer. PAID is a *derived* column: It derives as SUM(PAYAMT) from the column in the PAYMENTS table, and storing it in the CUSTOMERS table would be

EMP#	ENAME	DEPT#	HIREDATE
100	Spenser	E21	06-19-1980
110	Lucchessi	A00	05-16-1958
120	O'Connell	A00	12-05-1963
130	Quintana	C01	07-28-1971
140	Nicholls	C01	12-15-1976
150	Adamson	D11	02-12-1972
160	Pianka	D11	10-11-1977
290	Parker	D31	05-30-1980
300	Smith	D31	06-19-1972
310	Setright	D31	09-12-1964

EMP

EMP#	SALARY
100	26150
110	38170
120	37950
130	33800
140	35420
150	30280
160	27250
290	15340
310	15900

SAL_EMP

EMP#	COMMISSION
300	17750
290	4780
310	3200

COM_EMP

Figure 8.10. *Entity Subtype-Supertype Relationship*

redundant. Such redundancy must be controlled by an explicit integrity constraint (see Section 8.3.4) to guarantee consistency.

A more subtle type of derived information is sometimes employed for entity subtype-supertype relationships (see Chapter 6). In the design in Figure 8.10, the common attributes of the entity supertype Employee are recorded in the base table EMP, and the attribute unique to the entity supertypes Salaried-Employee and Commissioned-Employee are recorded in the SAL_EMP and COM_EMP base tables respectively (either or both salary and commission are possible for an employee).

Note that whether an employee earns a salary and/or commission is represented by the *foreign keys and referential constraints*. Indeed, that is precisely the information used to derive the join views for the two entity subtypes (see Chapter 6).

Consider now the column ETYPE added to the EMP entity supertype base table, shown in Figure 8.11. It takes the values S for salary, C for commission, and B for both. Such a column seems convenient for certain queries. For example, retrieving information about salaried or commissioned employees that *does not include the salary or commission themselves* could be achieved by using a simpler restrict table operation on ETYPE, rather than the join operation of EMP with either SAL_EMP or COM_EMP that would be required without ETYPE.

EMP#	ENAME	DEPT#	HIREDATE	ETYPE
100	Spenser	E21	06-19-1980	S
110	Lucchessi	A00	05-16-1958	S
120	O'Connell	A00	12-05-1963	S
130	Quintana	C01	07-28-1971	S
140	Nicholls	C01	12-15-1976	S
150	Adamson	D11	02-12-1972	S
160	Pianka	D11	10-11-1977	S
290	Parker	D31	05-30-1980	B
300	Smith	D31	06-19-1972	C
310	Setright	D31	09-12-1964	B

EMP

Figure 8.11. *Derived Column and Redundancy*

But ETYPE is essentially a derived column: The information it conveys is already represented by the foreign keys and ETYPE derives from them. This redundancy must be controlled by additional integrity constraints (see Section 8.3.4) to guarantee that the derived column and the information from which it is derived are consistent.

8.2.7 Redundancy Control

8.2.7.1 Denormalized Designs

Because JDs are the most general type of column dependency, of which both MVDs and FDs are special cases, tables without JDs exhibit no redundancy due to column dependencies. Such tables, said to be "fully normalized," represent only one entity type, and all nonkey columns are dependent on the key, the whole key, and nothing but the key of their table and do not suffer from update anomalies. Full normalization, then, minimizes the potential for inconsistencies and, thus, the integrity burden on users and the DBMS (see Chapter 5). Conversely, tables that are less than fully normalized represent mixtures of entity types. The ensuing redundancy and anomalies impose additional integrity burden of controlling it on both the DBMS and users.

Note very carefully that only when it is devoid of any inconsistency—that is, *only if all redundancy is controlled*—can a table that is *not* fully normalized be recovered by joining its 5NF projections *without loss of information*. This nonloss recovery condition can be expressed formally as a table equality, namely

```
T = T{C1,...,Ci} JOIN ... T{Cj,...,Cn} JOIN ...
```

where T is a less than fully normalized table with columns C1–Cn and the T{}s are its 5NF projections. In fact, the table equality condition is essentially the additional integrity constraint, which must be enforced for each less than fully normalized table T at all times to control redundancy and guarantee consistency and, thus, to prevent loss of information. For example, for the 3NF table ASSIGNS in Figure 8.8 (T=ASSIGNS), the integrity constraint to control redundancy is

```
assigns = ASSIGNS{emp#,project} JOIN ASSIGNS{emp#,activity}
```

where ASSIGNS{} are 5NF projections of ASSIGNS. Similarly, for the 4NF table ASSIGNS in Figure 8.9

```
assigns = ASSIGNS{emp#,project} JOIN
          ASSIGNS{project,activity} JOIN ASSIGNS{emp#,activity}
```

To enforce this type of table equality constraint the DBMS must perform, for every update, a relational **table comparison** check: It must compare the after-update version of the table to the after-update join of its 5NF projection to determine if the update violates the constraint, that is, if the table is not equal to the joins. If it does, the DBMS must reject the update (see Chapter 2).

8.2.7.2 Derived Information

In the PAYMENTS case in the previous section, the following additional integrity constraint must be explicitly declared and enforced for all updates on the table, such that they are propagated correctly through to PAID in CUSTOMERS, namely

```
CUSTOMERS(paid) = PAYMENTS(SUM(payamt))
```

In the employee case (see Figure 8.11), several additional constraints must be declared (they can be merged using AND into one, more complex constraint; see Section 8.3.3) as follows

- Any COM_EMP row must have a corresponding row in EMP with an ETYPE column of 'C' or 'B'

- Any EMP with an ETYPE column of 'C' or 'B' must have a corresponding row in COM_EMP

- Any SAL_EMP row must have a corresponding row in EMP with an ETYPE value of 'S' or 'B'

- Any EMP with an ETYPE value of 'S' or 'B' must have a corresponding row in SAL_EMP

8.3 Practical Implications

8.3.1 SQL and Keyless Tables

Even though in standard SQL and its commercially implemented dialects keys are optional—a serious flaw—users can readily avoid duplicate rows and the complications they cause (see Chapter 4) by defining a candidate key for every base table (see Chapter 3).

> ❖ **Note:** Keyless tables cause complications beyond duplicates. Unfortunately, the implementation of key support in SQL DBMSs has complexities and deficiencies that cannot be avoided, even if all base tables have keys (see next section).

8.3.2 SQL and Cross-Table Duplicates

SQL and its commercial implementations have weak (and complicated) integrity support. Constraint inheritance by derived tables (see Chapter 2) is not supported, and for that reason, most SQL DBMSs do not permit updates of multitable views, defeating one of the most important practical benefits from relational technology, **logical data independence** [1] (some SQL implementations support certain join view updates, but in an ad hoc manner, which cannot guarantee consistency in all circumstances).

The best users can do is to enforce integrity constraints on views via **stored procedures**—inferior to declarative integrity (see Chapter 2)—if the DBMS supports them or, worse, by means of application code if it does not. This means that the *users* must formulate the constraints themselves [3,5] and make sure that they guarantee correctness, a task that the DBMS is in a much better position to perform [1]. All the more reason to adhere to the principle of orthogonal design [3] and avoid cross-table duplicates (see Chapter 4).

8.3.3 SQL and "Denormalization"

Due to numerous flaws in the design and implementation of SQL, the performance of SQL DBMSs is often less than what it should and could be, leading users to "denormalize for performance." Even if arguments for denormalization were not questionable [6] (or outright fallacious [1]), this approach would require, as part of the data language's integrity support, the ability to declare the additional constraints necessary to control the redundancy produced by denormalization; and DBMS enforcement of those constraints.

But SQL and its commercial implementations make it very difficult, to put it mildly, to express constraints (see Chapter 2). Consider, for example, the table equality constraint for table ASSIGNS in Figure 8.8. It should be possible to declare it as follows

```
CREATE ASSERTION denorm_assigns
  CHECK assigns = ((SELECT emp#,project
                    FROM assigns)
                JOIN
                  (SELECT emp#,activity
                   FROM assigns);
```

But SQL does not support direct table comparison operations. The indirect SQL formulation would look something like the following [7]:

```
CREATE ASSERTION denorm_assigns
  CHECK (NOT EXISTS
        (SELECT DISTINCT emp#,project,activity
        FROM assigns AS a1
        WHERE NOT EXISTS
            (SELECT DISTINCT emp#,project,activity
             FROM ((SELECT DISTINCT emp#,project
                    FROM assigns) AS p1
              NATURAL JOIN
             (SELECT DISTINCT emp#,activity
              FROM assigns) AS p2)) AS a2
             WHERE a1.emp# = a2.emp#
               AND a1.project = a2.project
               AND a1.activity = a2.activity)
             AND (NOT EXISTS
                  (SELECT DISTINCT emp#,project,activity
                   FROM ((SELECT DISTINCT emp#,project
                          FROM assigns) AS p1
                      NATURAL JOIN
                      (SELECT DISTINCT emp#,activity
                       FROM assigns) AS p2)) AS a2
                   WHERE NOT EXISTS
                       (SELECT DISTINCT emp#,project,activity
                        FROM assigns AS a1
                        WHERE a1.emp# = a2.emp#
                          AND a1.project = a2.project
                          AND a1.activity = a2.activity));
```

This expression for multivalued dependencies reduces to more simple ones for functional dependencies, for example, the table PROJMGR in Figure 8.7, which has a single simple key

```
CREATE ASSERTION denorm_projmgr
  CHECK (NOT EXISTS
        (SELECT *
         FROM projmgr AS x
         WHERE EXISTS
               (SELECT *
                FROM projmgr y
                WHERE x.pmgr# = y.pmgr#
                  AND x.dept# <> y.dept#)));
```

but becomes even *more* complex for join dependencies due to composite keys; this is yet another reason to define simple surrogate keys (see Chapter 3).

8.3.4 SQL and Derived Information

For the simple PAYMENTS example in Section 8.2.6, the additional constraint necessary to ensure that the derived PAID values in CUSTOMERS and the PAYAMT values in PAYMENTS are consistent can be expressed in standard SQL as

```
CREATE ASSERTION derived_info
  CHECK (NOT EXISTS
        (SELECT *
         FROM customers c, payments p
         WHERE c.cust# = p.cust#
           AND SUM(p.payamt) NOT IN
                             (SELECT paid
                              FROM customers));
```

For the employees case in Figure 8.11, four constraints—not too convoluted, but long and potentially expensive to enforce—would have to be declared. The four constraints can be merged into one, but this makes the expression somewhat more prone to error and more difficult to debug.

```
*/Any COM_EMP row must have a corresponding row in EMP with a
*/ETYPE column of 'C' or 'B'
CREATE ASSERTION check1
  CHECK (NOT EXISTS
        (SELECT *
          FROM com_emp
          WHERE emp# NOT IN
                    (SELECT emp#
                     FROM emp
                     WHERE ETYPE IN ('C', 'B'))));

*/Any EMP with a ETYPE column of 'C' or 'B' must have a
*/corresponding row in COM_EMP
CREATE ASSERTION check2
  CHECK (NOT EXISTS
        (SELECT *
          FROM emp
          WHERE ETYPE IN ('C', 'B')
            AND emp# NOT IN
                    (SELECT emp#
                     FROM com_emp)));

*/Any SAL_EMP row must have a corresponding row in EMP with a
*/ETYPE column of 'S' or 'B'
CREATE ASSERTION check3
  CHECK (NOT EXISTS
        (SELECT *
          FROM sal_emp
          WHERE emp# NOT IN
                    (SELECT emp#
                     FROM emp
                     WHERE ETYPE IN ('S', 'B'))));
```

```
*/Any EMP with a ETYPE column of 'S' or 'B' must have a
*/corresponding row in SAL_EMP
CREATE ASSERTION check4
  CHECK (NOT EXISTS
        (SELECT *
         FROM emp
         WHERE ETYPE IN
                      ('S', 'B')
                   AND emp# NOT IN
                            (SELECT emp#
                             FROM sal_emp)));
```

Two of the constraints cannot avoid subsuming the referential constraints, which means that the DBMS will check those constraints *twice*, once as referential constraints and once in the additional constraints to control redundancy. In large and complex databases with numerous constraints, redundant checking may well defeat one of the purposes for which columns such as ETYPE are added in the first place—performance. The other purpose—query simplification—can be achieved with views, which avoids the integrity complications (for the correct solution in this specific case see Chapter 6).

However, all this is moot because SQL DBMSs do not currently support ASSERTIONs (the standard does permit the declaration of constraints as CHECK conditions in CREATE TABLE statements, but this is not the best idea for constraints that span multiple tables). This means that users must resort to stored procedures or, worse, application code to control redundancy.

8.4 Conclusion and Recommendations

Sometimes there are sound business or technical reasons for [duplicating] stored data. However . . . such redundancy should be carefully controlled—that is, the DBMS should be aware of it, if it exists, and should assume responsibility for . . . guarantee[ing] that

> the database is never inconsistent as seen by the user by ensuring that any change made to [any of the redundant] entries is automatically applied to the other one also. [2]

If redundancy is introduced in the database but is not controlled by the DBMS, users would "ha[ve] to know that [they are] responsible for keeping things 'in sync'; [otherwise] certain queries can produce inconsistencies and contradictions" [2]. With large and complex databases, this approach has a high risk of errors of omission or commission. The price to be paid for redundancy is severe: Additional integrity constraints must be declared and checked to control it, which would otherwise be unnecessary (see Chapters 3 and 8). SQL DBMSs exacerbate it by making the necessary constraints prohibitively difficult, or even impossible to express; neither do they have the intelligence to integrate constraint checks into their overall optimization strategy. Checking a large number of such constraints may well have a significant impact of its own on performance, possibly defeating the very purpose for which denormalization is usually undertaken in the first place. Whether and when the effect of denormalization is advantageous (if at all) depends on many *implementation* details and circumstances (the specific DBMS, database physical design, hardware configuration, application and access mix, and so on), which is precisely where performance issues should be addressed.

Given SQL's poor design, even with very simple tables, the probability of even sophisticated users *(a)* coming up with the complex constraint formulations, *(b)* doing so without errors, *(c)* knowing whether they are valid in SQL, and *(d)* debugging them if they are erroneous or invalid, is practically nil. Besides, SQL DBMSs do not support ASSERTIONs anyway. Because constraints can only be defined procedurally or, worse, via application code rather than declaratively, the endeavor is so prohibitive that it is simply not performed. The consequences are predictable:

> *Finished testing a COBOL program for a software company whose main product is a well-known government contract accounting system . . . Now the [expletive deleted] database . . . is replete with repeating groups, redundant fields, etc. On top of all that, because it is one of the central files to the entire system, there are literally hundreds of rules and relationships, all of which must be enforced by the dozens of subprograms that access it. I found so many violations of so many of these rules in this new subprogram that I filled five single-spaced pages with comments and suggestions. And I probably missed [the more obscure problems]. Several [such problems], perhaps.*
> —ONLINE MESSAGE

It is, therefore, hard to see how "denormalization" or the redundant storing of derived information can be deemed "practical" if, on top of the many constraints imposed by the multiplicity of business rules in the real world, users would have to declare *additional constraints for every "denormalized" table*, many of which can be horrendously complex. The only way in which denormalized designs and other redundancies can be justified is by ignoring, as is usually the case, the integrity implications, which is tantamount to accepting almost certain data corruption and/or incorrect query results (see Chapter 5).

Just say no.

References

[1]   F. Pascal, *Understanding Relational Databases*, New York, NY: John Wiley & Sons, 1993.

[2]   C. J. Date, *An Introduction to Database Systems*, 6th ed., Reading, MA: Addison-Wesley, 1998.

[3]   C. J. Date, "Updating Union, Intersection and Difference Views," *Relational Database Writings 1991–1994*, Reading, MA: Addison-Wesley, 1995.

[4]   C. J. Date, "A New Database Design Principle," *Relational Database Writings 1991–1994*, Reading, MA: Addison-Wesley, 1995.

[5]   C. J. Date, "Updating Joins and Other Views," *Relational Database Writings 1991–1994*, Reading, MA: Addison-Wesley, 1995.

[6]   C. J. Date, "The Normal Is So . . . Interesting," Parts 1–2, *Database Programming and Design*, November and December 1997.

[7]   C. J. Date, personal communication, 1999.

[8]   J. Reeder, "Denormalize at Your Own Risk," *InfoDB*, Fall 1989.

[9]   C. J. Date, "Normalization Is Not Panacea," *Database Programming and Design*, April 1998.

[10] C. J. Date, "The Final Normal Form!" Parts 1–2, *Database Programming and Design*, January and February 1998.

Will SQL Come
to Order: Quota Queries

*Does anyone know of a SQL query that will allow me to select the top
ten sales[people] from my SALES table? I can't think of anything, [and]
even desperate attempts like*

```
SELECT emp#
FROM sales
WHERE COUNT(*) < 11
ORDER BY sales_amt
```

*don't work . . . I tried ROWID, and just can't seem to get anything to
work . . . [ultimately I had to] . . . ORDER BY sales amount, count the top
10 and set a sales amount > 'amount' [WHERE] criterion before printing
the report . . . would like to know how to do it with any SQL system. It
seems like a common thing to want to do.*

—ONLINE MESSAGE

9.1 The Issue

"Quota queries" are common in database practice. There is a table
operation underlying them, but SQL and its commercial implementations do not support it in the most direct, simple, and intuitive way.
Consequently, users find it hard to express such queries in a way that
guarantees correct results.

This chapter

- Conceptualizes the table operation for quota queries

- Describes a simple and intuitive way to express it

- Assesses critically the SQL approach, including the correct
  formulation

9.2 Fundamentals

Consider the SALES table in Figure 9.1 and the query: "What are the top q salesmen?" where q is an integer quota.

Suppose q=3. When the table is short and the quota is small (here, four and three), it is easy to calculate the answer mentally. There are at least two procedures that can be employed. One is

- Select the row with the maximum SALE_AMT value

- Select the row with the maximum SALE_AMT value from the remaining rows

- Select the row with the maximum SALE_AMT value from the remaining rows

Another is

- Sort the rows in SALE_AMT order

- Select the first three rows

Both procedures yield the result in Figure 9.2.

Such mental procedures become prohibitive, however, with very long tables and large quotas, which is why they are better left to a DBMS.

ENAME	SALE_AMT
Johnson	18270
Marino	33800
Adamson	30280
Thompson	41250

Figure 9.1. *SALES Table*

ENAME	SALE_AMT
Thompson	41250
Marino	33800
Adamson	30280

Figure 9.2. *Top Three Salesmen*

Note, however, that whatever *execution procedure* is used—of which there can be more than one—the *logical table operation involved* and thus the result of the quota query must always be the same.

> [The table operation] splits, or partitions a table in two. One [part] has the cardinality of the quota—the result—and [the other is a] leftover that is discarded. . . . How [the] operation is expressed *syntactically* to the DBMS depends on the design of the data language . . . Since there are several [execution] procedures that the DBMS can [choose from], whose performance will vary [with specific tables and quotas], the [syntax] should not force a[ny] particular one... If the DBMS were designed to understand [the] partitioning semantics ("split SALES into two sets of rows, such that one has the q highest SALES values") [and the statement were *nonprocedural*, the DBMS optimizer could choose the best performing one in every case, using database statistics]. [1]

9.2.1 Ambiguities

Before going into syntax, however, there are two slight complications that table operation underlying quota queries must contend with. The first and more straightforward is a quota greater than the number of rows in the table (or cardinality), that is, q>N where N is the table cardinality. It makes sense in such cases for the DBMS to output *all N rows.*

Second, if the table contains ties, quota queries can be ambiguous. Consider, for example, the table in Figure 9.3 (sorted in SALE_AMT order for convenience).

With N=7, for q=1, the result is the row {Thompson,41250}. But for q=2, there are two options:

- Strict adherence to the quota; include in the result only one of the rows tied on 33,800

- Go over the quota; include both tied rows

This dilemma also applies to q=5,6. What should the DBMS do in such cases? If the DBMS opted for the first alternative, it would have no logical basis for preferring either of the tied rows to the other, which in practical terms means that it would choose arbitrarily, possibly yielding a different result at different times (see Figure 9.4) *depending on the execution procedure.* It may make more sense, therefore, for the DBMS to go over the quota and always include *all* tied rows.

ENAME	SALE_AMT
Thompson	41250
Marino	33800
Quintana	33800
Adamson	30280
Johnson	18270
Jones	18270
Shaw	18270

Figure 9.3. *SALES Table with Ties*

ENAME	SALE_AMT
Thompson	41250
Marino	33800

ENAME	SALE_AMT
Thompson	41250
Quintana	33800

Figure 9.4. *Different Possible Results for Same Query*

❖ **Note:** A result including only one of the tied rows actually yields the top q *sale amounts*, not salespersons. Given that the entity type represented by the table is Salesperson (the propositions represented by the rows are about salespersons), a query about entities of a different type would have to be formulated accordingly. The key identifies salespersons, *not sale amounts*, so it should not be part of the result, in which case the ties would be irrelevant. Thus, for q=3

SALE_AMT
41250
33800
30280

Figure 9.5 contains the correct results for quota queries on the SALES table for q=1,2,3,4,5,6,7+.

9.2.2 The Declarative Solution

What exactly must the DBMS know to execute the table operation underlying quota queries correctly?

- Name of the table
- Quota q (the cardinality of the result)
- Name of the quota-column
- Quota type (top or bottom)

ENAME	SALE_AMT
Thompson	41250
Marino	33800
Quintana	33800

q=2,3

ENAME	SALE_AMT
Thompson	41250

q=1

ENAME	SALE_AMT
Thompson	41250
Marino	33800
Quintana	33800
Adamson	30280
Johnson	18270
Jones	18270
Shaw	18270

q>=5

ENAME	SALE_AMT
Thompson	41250
Marino	33800
Quintana	33800
Adamson	30280

q=4

Figure 9.5. *Results for Queries with q=1-4,5+*

The data language must permit the user to convey this information to the DBMS.

The original data language developed by the inventor of the relational model did support quota query expressions directly as follows:

```
GET W(q) (sales.ename,sales.saleamt):DOWN sales.saleamt
```

where q is the quota and DOWN stands for top quota [2]. Along the same lines, a slightly refined, formal syntax has been proposed more recently [3]:

```
rel-exp QUOTA (q, q-column, ASC|DESC)
```

where:

rel-exp is a table name, or table expression

q = quota

q-column = quota column

ASC|DESC = bottom|top quota

Thus, for q=3 top quota on SALES

```
sales QUOTA (3,sale_amt,DESC)
```

Such expressions are simple and intuitive. And because they are *non-procedural*—they specify the desired result, not how to obtain it—the DBMS is left to its own devices—the optimizer—to choose the best performing execution procedure.

9.3 Practical Implications

9.3.1 SQL and Quota Queries

The average user finds it difficult to formulate quota queries in one simple, intuitive expression because SQL does not provide one. To avoid the much less desirable application code option, users attempt all sorts of "desperate" workarounds. For example, some commercial DBMSs generate quasi-columns that seem, on the face of it, useful for quota queries. One is ROWNUM, whose values reflect the order of rows in a result

```
SELECT ename, sale_amt
FROM sales
WHERE ROWNUM <= q
ORDER BY sale_amt DESC
```

But ORDER BY operates on the *result* of the SELECT expression, which is (partially) determined by the WHERE clause, which in turn references ROWNUM. And because ROWNUM values are established *after* the ordering, such queries are circular and will not terminate until the result set is empty.

❖ **Note:** Statements using *implicit* database information, such as system-generated quasi-columns ROWNUM (or ROWID, see next example), can hardly be considered intuitive because the user must be aware of the existence and meaning of such information and figure out its applicability to the specific type of query under consideration. ROWNUM was never intended for quota queries and most users are unlikely to consider it. Also very instructive is the claim by one reviewer of this book's manuscript:

> *The problem of assigning ROWNUM values prior to application of the ORDER BY clause is no longer an issue . . . you can create a view with an ORDER BY clause, then retrieve the first ROWNUM rows from the view, as in this example:*

```
SELECT *
FROM sales;
```

EMP#	SALES
1	120000
2	20000
3	15000
4	15000
5	95000

```
CREATE OR REPLACE VIEW sales_view
   AS SELECT emp#,sales
      FROM sales
      ORDER BY sales DESC;
```

```
SELECT *
FROM sales_view
WHERE rownum < 3;
```

EMP#	SALES
1	120000
5	95000

—REVIEW OF THIS BOOK'S MANUSCRIPT

But, first, this solution is procedural—it requires *three* SQL statements. Second and more important, because row order is inessential in a relational database, ORDER BY is not a database operation, but rather a presentation—and, thus, application—function (it is nothing but the creation of a physical index for the table). View definitions using this clause produce views with **essential ordering**, which violate relational closure; such views may lose the information embedded in the ordering when they are operated upon (e.g., joined with other tables) or reordered for performance optimization purposes.

Another implicit quasi-column generated by the same commercial database system, ROWID, has values that represent, via a complex function of row physical address, the order of rows in storage; otherwise put, ROWIDs are *physical pointers.* Exposing them to users and applications violates **physical data independence**, with serious practical consequences beyond those due to implicitness. Subject to implementation changes, ROWIDs may not always reflect correct or sufficient information on the desired result order or, if they do, extracting the order may be quite complex [4]. If and when the database is physically reorganized—which may be desirable for optimization—such information will be lost. Moreover, in most SQL DBMSs only base tables are physically stored and, consequently, ROWIDs cannot be used in queries against views because, as virtual rows, view rows do not have physical addresses. Such artificial distinctions between stored and derived tables (which are base and which are virtual is a database design decision and, in that sense, arbitrary and subject to change) violate the relational spirit in which "all tables are created equal."

One SQL dialect offers a ROWCOUNT function, which restricts results
to a certain quota, for example

```
SET ROWCOUNT q
GO
SELECT ename, sale_amt
FROM sales
ORDER BY sale_amt DESC
GO
```

But the DBMS enforces the quota by retrieving the whole table and
arbitrarily discarding all rows beyond the first q, hardly an efficient
solution. Note also that with this formulation, the treatment of ties is
not defined to the user.

> ❖ **Note:** Another formulation is proposed
>
> ```
> SELECT ename, sale_amt
> FROM sales
> ORDER BY sale_amt DESC
> STOP AFTER q
> ```
>
> which suffers from a similar drawback. See previous note on ORDER BY.

Because of these deficiencies, none of these workarounds (which are
proprietary to boot) are correct, general solutions.

Consider now the SQL statement

```
SELECT a.ename,a.sale_amt
FROM sales a,sales b
WHERE a.sale_amt <= b.sale_amt
GROUP BY a.ename,a.sale_amt
HAVING COUNT(*) <= q
ORDER BY a.sale_amt
```

Even ignoring the ORDER BY clause, this expression is neither simple nor intuitive (including SQL's requirement that SALES also be included in the GROUP BY clause because it is not an aggregate column). Even when looking at it, it is not obvious that it yields the top q sales and why, so few users would come up with it. Indeed, it was proposed by one very skilled SQL developer after "a couple of hours to develop and test," who conceded that "it was the most complicated step among those that I developed that day." It is also somewhat procedural, forcing an explicit self-join, grouping and sorting sequence, which SQL optimizers may be inhibited from transforming into a more efficient execution (see Chapter 4). What's more, this formulation still fails to produce correct results for all q's. Figure 9.6 shows that for q=2,5,6, instead of including all tied rows in the result, it chooses to *exclude* all of them.

The same criticisms apply to the following similar formulation, which, significantly, was the third one following *two erroneous* attempts [3]:

```
SELECT a.ename,a.sale_amt
FROM sales a,sales b
WHERE a.sale_amt < b.sale_amt
  OR a.ename=b.ename
GROUP BY a.ename,a.sale_amt
HAVING 3>= COUNT(*)
ORDER BY a.sale_amt DESC
```

ENAME	SALE_AMT
Thompson	41250

q=2

ENAME	SALE_AMT
Thompson	41250
Marino	33800
Quintana	33800
Adamson	30280

q=5,6

Figure 9.6. *Results for q=2,5,6*

Obviously, "It's easy to lose your way in SQL queries that involve Cartesian products of tables with themselves together with GROUP BYs and SELECTs that refer to one side of such a product, HAVINGs that refer to the other, and 'backward comparisons' such as q <= COUNT(*) instead of COUNT(*) >= q" [3].

> ❖ **Note:** The need for backward comparison may have been eliminated in subsequent revisions of the SQL standard, but for backward compatibility reasons such quirks must be retained by languages, causing language redundancy with its own set of problems [1].

It is argued that if the English formulation is recast into the more precise: "Find all salespersons SX such that the number of salespersons with lower sales than SY is less than q," the *correct* SQL expression (which, incidentally, was not valid prior to the SQL:92 standard) can be derived directly from it.

```
SELECT sx.ename,sx.sale_amt
FROM sales sx
WHERE (SELECT COUNT(*)
       FROM sales sy
       WHERE sy.sale_amt < sx.sale_amt) < q
```

This, purportedly, "is much easier to understand and very much less error-prone than GROUP BY and HAVING" expressions, in part because it is "actually a fairly direct transliteration of its relational calculus counterpart" [4]:

```
sx.ename WHERE COUNT(sy WHERE sy.sale_amt < sx.sale_amt) < q
```

Whether this expression is more intuitive is in the eye of the beholder. The other SQL expressions are *so* unintuitive that, indeed, anything else is better. But the fact remains that the average user does not come by it readily, which suggests that users do not recast queries this way. The simple QUOTA shorthand would be much easier and intuitive for users and easier for a DBMS to optimize.

9.4 Conclusion and Recommendations

Even though it is possible to express quota queries in SQL, the correct formulation is not intuitive and not as optimizable as it should be. Furthermore, there are more complex SQL expressions that may yield incorrect results or even fail to produce any rows at all [3]. This is not due to lack of better syntax, but simply because SQL was not designed to support it directly. One commercial DBMS, which is currently somewhat of an orphan, can express quota queries as follows [5]:

```
FOR FIRST q x IN sales
SORTED BY x.sales DESC
PRINT x.ename, x.sales
```

Although proprietary and somewhat more verbose, it is still simpler, more direct, and intuitive than the SQL equivalent. It is, however, unclear if it correctly disambiguates in the presence of ties and what is the quality of its optimization is.

As is usually the case, problems in practice derive not from SQL DBMSs being relational, but rather from poor language design, weak or no relational support, or implementation flaws.

Adherence to relational principles—in this case, relational calculus—and proper modeling of the business reality of interest, guarantee expressions that yield correct results. Users would benefit from educating themselves in relational algebra and/or calculus. Otherwise, they must memorize the proper SQL syntax and use it exclusively to avoid wrong answers.

References

[1] F. Pascal, *Understanding Relational Databases*, New York, NY: John Wiley & Sons, 1993.

[2] F. Pascal, "Will SQL Come to Order?" Parts 1–2, *SQL Forum*, July/August and September/October 1992.

[3] C. J. Date, "Quota Queries," Parts 1–3, *Relational Database Writings 1994–1997*, Reading, MA: Addison-Wesley, 1998.

[4] C. J. Date, personal communication, 1999.

[5] Product documentation.

What You Don't Know Can Hurt You: Missing Information

I am hoping someone can explain these results:

```
SELECT COUNT(*)
FROM customer -->154168

SELECT COUNT(*)
FROM customer
WHERE salutation = "mr" --> 4338

SELECT COUNT(*)
FROM customer
WHERE salutation<> "mr" --> 6269
```

Why does the sum of the last two statements not equal the count in the first statement?

—ONLINE MESSAGE

The "SQL Language Reference" manual contradicts itself right away with the definition of NULL.

```
Null is not equivalent to zero or to blank...
Empty strings have a null value...
```

In subsequent section "Nulls and search conditions," the manual doesn't distinguish NULL and zero-length string. It goes on to explain that

```
SELECT ... WHERE x IS NULL;
```

returns null rows as well as empty strings. The problem is, the converse is not true. Such a statement is guaranteed to return nothing

```
SELECT ... WHERE x = ''
```

This is a very nasty exception! Some further confusion in the manual can be found in the following:

If any item in an expression contains a null value, then the result of evaluating the expression is null.

However, this doesn't seem to apply to NULL string. These expressions simply treat NULL as empty strings.

```
@length(x)
'[' || x || ']'
```

Furthermore, x IS NULL never results in null! It seems the vendor has major confusion on NULL.
—ONLINE MESSAGE

Q: What are the space and performance issues pertaining to the use of nulls? From my performance and tuning class days, one wants to use "NOT NULL" when possible. Why was that, and more importantly, is that still the case?

A: Internally, any nullable column is treated as variable-length, including "fixed size" types like INT (null internally is INT and variable length). There's a degree of overhead involved in figuring the length, and a bit of extra space required to maintain the length, as well as the data per se. You have to weigh this against the space savings. You do give up "update in place" but you said it's not a consideration.
—ONLINE EXCHANGE

10.1 The Issue

As attested to by the volume of writings and the heat of the debate on the subject (see references)—without an end in sight—how to treat missing information has possibly been the thorniest aspect of database management. Users are left between a rock and a hard place: They can either rely on SQL's problematic version of three-valued logic based on

NULLs and risk hard to interpret database answers and/or hard to detect errors in query results or take upon themselves the burden of what is a complex database function, which belongs in the DBMS.

This chapter

- Makes the important distinction between inapplicable and missing information by clarifying their underlying different semantics (meaning)

- Provides design guidelines for the avoidance of the former and the minimization of the latter

- Describes the metadata approach to missing information

- Discusses DBMS support requirements and their implications for users and vendors

- Demonstrates the drawbacks of the many-valued logic approach to missing information

- Assesses SQL's support of three-valued logic (3VL) via NULLs

- Draws conclusions and offers practical recommendations

10.2 Fundamentals

As reiterated throughout this book, databases are *structured* (that is, organized) collections of propositions about some segment of interest in the real world. Propositions are assertions of fact about real-world entities. For example, the following is a proposition about entities of type Employee:

> *Employee identified by employee* number **100**, *named* **Spenser**, *works in department* **E21**, *was hired on* **6/19/1980**, *earns a salary of* **$26,150**

Relational databases use tables to organize (structure) the representation of propositions. The propositions are represented by sets of values—rows—and columns, which represent sets of values of the attributes of those entities in the real world. For example, the table in Figure 10.1 represents propositions about employees. The previous proposition is represented by the first row.

> ❖ **Note:** Informally rows can be viewed as representing the entities themselves, narrowly defined as collections of attribute values of interest. Thus, in Figure 10.1 the rows can be viewed as representing employees. Rows of *base* tables seem more amenable to this conceptualization than *derived* tables, such as views, but rows of views can be viewed as more *abstract* entities of interest.

Propositions about the real world are either true or false. If database management adheres to this **two-valued logic** (2VL) nature of the real world, starting with a set of true propositions—**axioms**—and using formal **rules of inference**, additional propositions, **theorems**, can be derived that are also true. In database terms, additional rows can be derived by table operations from an initial set of rows, which is exactly

EMP#	NAME	DEPT#	HIREDATE	SALARY
100	Spenser	E21	06-19-1980	26150
110	Lucchessi	A00	05-16-1958	38170
120	O'Connell	A00	12-05-1963	37950
130	Quintana	C01	07-28-1971	33800
240	Marino	D21	12-05-1979	33760
250	Smith	D21	10-30-1969	39180
260	Johnson	D21	09-11-1975	17250
290	Parker	D31	05-30-1980	15340
310	Setright	D31	09-12-1964	15900

Figure 10.1. *Representation of Propositions about Employees*

what querying is [1]. The derived rows will represent true propositions, however, *if and only if*

- The initial set of rows represents propositions that are true
- Table operations obey the formal inference rules of 2VL

Otherwise, correctness of query results—the truth of derived propositions—cannot be guaranteed.

10.2.1 Meaningless Assertions

Suppose that some, but not all, employees earn a commission on top of their salary and consider the not uncommon table design in Figure 10.2. The commission amount for employees who do not earn a commission is *not assertable*. The column COMMISSION, therefore, represents an attribute that those employees do not possess in the real world. Therefore, *no values are missing here*: COMMISSION values *do not apply* to salary-only employee rows.

Out of a set of six attributes, then, five are common to all entities and one is unique to only some of them. This indicates an entity

EMP#	NAME	DEPT#	HIREDATE	SALARY	COMMISSION
100	Spenser	E21	06-19-1980	26150	
110	Lucchessi	A00	05-16-1958	38170	
120	O'Connell	A00	12-05-1963	37950	
130	Quintana	C01	07-28-1971	33800	
240	Marino	D21	12-05-1979	33760	
250	Smith	D21	10-30-1969	39180	
260	Johnson	D21	09-11-1975	17250	
290	Parker	D31	05-30-1980	15340	4780
310	Setright	D31	09-12-1964	15900	3200

Figure 10.2. *Inapplicable Values Represented as Missing*

subtype-supertype relationship. The design in Figure 10.3 with one base table for the entity supertype common attributes and one for the entity subtype unique attribute is devoid of inapplicable values. The entity subtype maps to a join view (see Chapter 6).

10.2.2 Empty Assertions

Suppose now that the salary amount for some employees is unknown. In Figure 10.4, rows representing those employees have missing SALARY values.

SALARY values *do exist in the real world* for all employees, except that in Figure 10.4 some are really missing. What is not known cannot be asserted, so what facts do the rows with missing values represent? Consider Figure 10.5 with all nonkey values unknown. Few would dispute that it makes no sense to record such "full nothings" in databases, yet "partial nothings," such as those in Figure 10.4, are deemed useful in some way.

EMP#	NAME	DEPT#	HIREDATE	SALARY
100	Spenser	E21	06-19-1980	26150
110	Lucchessi	A00	05-16-1958	38170
120	O'Connell	A00	12-05-1963	37950
130	Quintana	C01	07-28-1971	33800
240	Marino	D21	12-05-1979	33760
250	Smith	D21	10-30-1969	39180
260	Johnson	D21	09-11-1975	17250
290	Parker	D31	05-30-1980	15340
310	Setright	D31	09-12-1964	15900

EMP

EMP#	COMMISSION
290	4780
310	3200

COM_EMP

Figure 10.3. *Representation without Inapplicable Values*

EMP#	NAME	DEPT#	HIREDATE	SALARY
100	Spenser	E21	06-19-1980	26150
110	Lucchessi	A00	05-16-1958	
120	O'Connell	A00	12-05-1963	37950
130	Quintana	C01	07-28-1971	33800
240	Marino	D21	12-05-1979	33760
250	Smith	D21	10-30-1969	
260	Johnson	D21	09-11-1975	
290	Parker	D31	05-30-1980	15340
310	Setright	D31	09-12-1964	15900

Figure 10.4. *Unknown Values Represented as Missing*

The argument seems to be that even though some salary amounts are unknown, it is nevertheless known that *all employees do earn a salary*. Note very carefully, though, that what is assertable, then, is not the salary amount, but the *existence* of a salary. Thus, only four values

EMP#	NAME	DEPT#	HIREDATE	SALARY
100				
110				
120				
130				
240				
250				
260				
290				
310				

Figure 10.5. *All Nonkey Values Unknown*

can be asserted for all employees: employee number, name, department, hire date, and the existence of a salary; the salary amount can be asserted only for employees with known salaries. In other words, there are two kinds of assertions here: propositions about all employees and propositions about employees with known salaries. For reasons similar—but not identical (see next section)—to those in the entity subtype-supertype case (see Chapter 6), by mapping the four common attributes to one table and salary to another, shown in Figure 10.6, both redundancy (see Chapter 8) and empty assertions are avoided.

10.2.3 Missing Information as Metadata

The case of unknown values resembles that of an entity subtype-supertype relationship—a combination of attributes common to all entities and attributes unique to some entities (see Chapter 6). Note very carefully, though, that in this case there *is no unique attribute*—salary is

EMP#	NAME	DEPT#	HIREDATE
100	Spenser	E21	06-19-1980
110	Lucchessi	A00	05-16-1958
120	O'Connell	A00	12-05-1963
130	Quintana	C01	07-28-1971
240	Marino	D21	12-05-1979
250	Smith	D21	10-30-1969
260	Johnson	D21	09-11-1975
290	Parker	D31	05-30-1980
310	Setright	D31	09-12-1964

EMP

EMP#	SALARY
100	26150
120	37950
130	33800
240	33760
290	15340
310	15900

EMP_SAL

Figure 10.6. *Representation without Missing Values*

common to all employees—and, therefore, there are no subtypes and supertype. Unlike the existence of a salary—which is an attribute of employees—*knowledge* of a salary amount is an attribute of the *salary amount*—whether it is known or not. It is, in other words, not data about the real world, but *data about the data*, or **metadata**. And representing both data and metadata in the same table would be a form of "bundling" more than one entity type into tables, which is known to cause complications (see Chapters 2, 8).

Where two bundled entity types are all real-world types, we separate them in two tables via further normalization (see Chapter 5). But what about metadata bundled with data?

10.2.4 DBMS Support

> The kind of data we are concerned with here is most commonly encountered in audit trails in which the source of the data, data entry operator ID, time of entry, and so on are captured. Extending an audit trail concept to include metadata about missing information would seem natural. To accomplish this goal, we would need to capture [for each table] . . . the primary key [value] of the row involved, a code classifying the data entry operator's belief, and an identifier for the column involved (but not a column value). This metadata can be recorded in separate lookup tables. While this solution can be implemented manually, why should not RDBMS products support audit trails in which the information to be captured is declaratively specified by the user? [2]

At table definition time, the DBMS could, for example, create a **meta-table** in the database catalog for each user database table and transparently record the pertinent missing information as users enter or update data in the tables. For example, a table SYS_EMP would be created in the catalog for the EMP table, and the DBMS would insert in it one row for each row that is entered in SAL, but not in EMP_SAL.

`SYS_EMP {PKVALUE,COLUMN,STATUS,...}`

The STATUS column could take values, such as UK (unknown), NV (not valid), NS (not supplied), and so on [2]. Additional information of interest could be added as desired (the user could be prompted at data entry time for this information). Figure 10.7 shows the rows of the metatable associated with the EMP table in Figure 10.6.

The DBMS would have, of course, to be aware of, understand, and maintain the relationships between data tables such as EMP and EMP_SAL and between them and the SYS_EMP metatable. It would have to update the metatables in the catalog transparently whenever the state of knowledge changes, for instance, when previously unknown values become known and are recorded in the data tables. For example, when the unknown salary of an employee becomes known, the row INSERT into SAL_EMP would trigger a row DELETE from SYS_EMP.

Table operations would also have to be modified to yield results with as many tables as there are types of propositions with only known values [2]. For example, a request for the number, name, and salary of all employees run against the two tables in Figure 10.6 should yield a result consisting not of the one table A with missing values in Figure 10.8, which is currently the case, but rather of the two tables

PKVALUE	COLUMN	STATUS
110	SALARY	UKN
250	SALARY	UKN
260	SALARY	UKN

SYS_EMP

Figure 10.7. *Missing Information as Metadata*

EMP#	NAME	SALARY
100	Spenser	26150
120	O'Connell	37950
130	Quintana	33800
240	Marino	33760
290	Parker	15340
310	Setright	15900

B1

EMP#	NAME	SALARY
110	Lucchessi	
100	Spenser	26150
120	O'Connell	37950
130	Quintana	33800
240	Marino	33760
250	Smith	
260	Johnson	
290	Parker	15340
310	Setright	15900

A

EMP#	NAME
110	Lucchessi
250	Smith
260	Johnson

B2

Figure 10.8. *Results with and without Missing Values*

B1 and B2, with the DBMS aware of the relationship between them for the purpose of further manipulation.

10.2.5 Many-Valued Logic

The likely reason for which the original relational model was revised to support two missing value marks, the **I-mark** for inapplicable values and the **A-mark** for applicable but unknown values, is that any value to be recorded in the database that cannot be specified falls in one of these two categories. Consider, for example, the following common cases [3]

- Value not valid; for example, unprevented integrity violation: unknown

- Value not supplied; for example, refusal to answer a question: unknown

- Value does not exist; for example, some employees do not earn a commission: inapplicable

- Value undefined; for example, average payment calculated by dividing total amount paid by number of payments made when no payments have yet been made: inapplicable

- Value is empty set; for example, outer-join of departments and employees tables where a department has no employees: inapplicable

Over time, an unspecifiable value of one type can become specifiable (e.g., an unknown value becomes known) or even convert to the other type (e.g., a noncommissioned employee starts earning an unknown commission). But at any point in time an unspecified value is *either* inapplicable or missing.

It should be clear at this point, however, that inapplicable or missing (unknown) values will occur in the database *if and only if* users record *(a)* meaningless assertions or *(b)* assertions that cannot be made because the facts are not known. Neither makes sense because, as already explained, in the real world, propositions are either true or false (2VL). So if users design databases (and vendors DBMSs) that adhere to 2VL—that is, they assert only what is assertable—there will be no inapplicable or missing values. Then *relational* database management guarantees correctness of query results because it is based on **first order predicate logic**, which, in turn, is grounded in 2VL.

If, on the other hand, both inapplicable or missing facts are also recorded, a **four-valued logic** (4VL) system will be required: true/false/ inapplicable/missing. Now, the I-Mark must be dispensed with because, as already explained, inapplicable values are not missing, but are a poor design artifact, which can and should be avoided. But missing values still require **three-valued logic** (3VL)—propositions are true/false/unknown. And the problem is that no generally agreed upon 3VL has been formulated that is internally consistent and as complete and intuitive as 2VL [3, 4, 5, 6, 7]. Moreover, "[even if] it would be possible to define a 3VL that is logically self-consistent . . . in a [database] system based on [it], certain conclusions will follow that are 'logically incorrect' in the real world" [6]. The numerous negative implications have been amply documented [2, 3, 5, 8], among them

- Propositions that are true in 3VL are not necessarily true in the real world.

- Tables that contain missing values are not relational tables; relational theory—including data manipulation—breaks down.

- Normalization rules (see Chapter 5) break down.

- A missing value mark is not a value and, thus, not of a data type and cannot be treated as a value by the DBMS (see Chapter 1).

- There are no criteria for treating missing values either as equal or not equal to one another.

Thus, any departure from the real world's 2VL will, unavoidably, result in some wrong database answers about the real world.

Note very carefully that a DBMS cannot prevent users from designing tables with inapplicable columns—the best it can do is discourage such practice by withholding support of I-marks and 4VL—so user discipline is required. If users introduce inapplicable values in the database and the DBMS supports only 3VL, incorrect answers to queries will ensue; for example: "Suppose employee Joe is not a salesperson and so does not qualify for a commission [value inapplicable]. Then Joe's commission [would] be misrepresented as 'value unknown'. . . One simple consequence of such misrepresentation is that Joe's total compensation (salary plus commission) will incorrectly evaluate to 'unknown' instead of to just the salary value" [3].

	2VL (n=2)	3VL (n=3)
Monadic operators	4	27
Dyadic operators	16	19,683

Figure 10.9. *Number of Logical Operators by Logic System*

Furthermore, any form of **many-valued logic** (that is, nVL where n > 2) complicates the data language—and, therefore, its implementation and use—enormously. To take just one example, consider the number of logical operators that must be supported by the data language. For nVL, n^n monadic operators (e.g., NOT) and n^{n^2} dyadic operators (e.g., =, AND) are necessary for completeness [9]. Figure 10.9 shows the number of operators required by 2VL and 3VL.

Extending a 2VL system to support 3VL is, therefore, nontrivial (not to mention prone to errors). Users will, consequently, not just have to contend with the complications of 3VL per se, but also with the consequences of the implementation errors they induce. SQL is a case in point.

10.3 Practical Implications

10.3.1 SQL NULLs

In standard SQL, an A-mark called NULL is used to represent a missing value. Therefore, SQL suffers from the problems inherent in 3VL as well as from many quirks, complications, counterintuitiveness, and outright errors [10, 11]; among them are the following:

- Aggregate functions (e.g., SUM(), AVG()) ignore NULLs (except for COUNT()).

- A scalar expression on a table without rows evaluates incorrectly to NULL, instead of 0.

- The expression "NULL=NULL" evaluates to NULL, but is actually invalid in SQL; yet ORDER BY treats NULLs as equal (whether they precede or follow "regular" values is left to the DBMS vendor).

- The expression "x IS NOT NULL" is not equal to "NOT(x IS NULL)," as is the case in 2VL.

- SQL's NOT does not mean the same as "not" in natural language [2] (for one of the consequences see the first quote at the beginning of this chapter).

- SQL's EXISTS does not behave like the 3VL EXISTS [12].

- Expressions evaluating to NULL are not deemed to violate integrity constraints (NULL is treated as true).

- Lack of support for the truth-valued domain, that is, a data type whose values are 'true' and 'false' (see Chapter 1); one consequence is that the literal NULL cannot appear in contexts in which any literals can appear; another is lack of support for all 27 monadic and 19,683 dyadic possible operators of 3VL [9].

> ❖ **Note:** Another example of how the NULL approach unnecessarily complicates the language is in Appendix 2A.

All commercially implemented SQL dialects follow this 3VL approach, and, thus, not only do they exhibit these problems, but they also have specific implementation problems, which vary across products.

10.3.2 User Options

Consider an ongoing real-world medical database that has been recording a large number of monthly birth variables for over twenty years. The (somewhat simplified) conceptual model is shown in Figure 10.10. Had the recording of all research variables started at the same time and continued

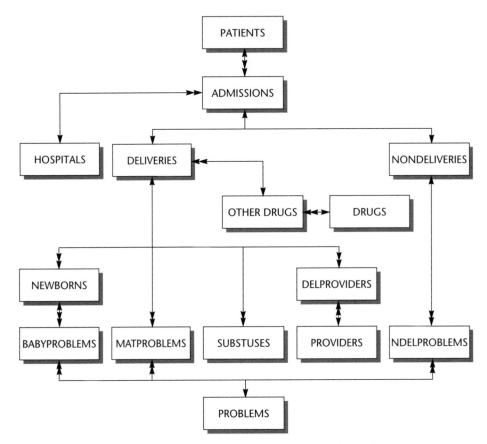

Figure 10.10. *Conceptual Model—Perinatal Database*

indefinitely, each entity type would have mapped to a base table and the pertinent variables (attributes) to columns. But new variables were continuously added and existing ones dropped at various points in time, so such a design would lead to a database full of NULLs.

10.3.2.1 NULLs and 4VL

Take, for example, the table ADMISSIONS, representing the Admission entity type in Figure 10.10. Six admission variables started on January 1976, when the database was initiated, but one, THOSP_ID, was added in March 1995. If the table were

```
ADMISSIONS {ADM#,PAT_ID,CLASS,SPONSOR,HOSP_ID,THOSP_ID}
```

the THOSP_ID column would represent an attribute that admissions prior to March 1995 do not possess, and, therefore, each row representing such an admission would have a NULL (inapplicable) in the THOSP_ID column. With hundreds of admissions per month, there would be hundreds of such NULLs. In the case of delivery variables—the bulk of the attributes—they were added as follows: 1/76, 1/78, 5/78, 1/80, 9/80, 10/80, 7/86, 8/89, 4/94, 3/95. A DELIVERIES table would also contain a very large (and growing) number of NULLs.

Because values in any column can also be unknown, two types of marks would be required to distinguish between missing and inapplicable values, as well as support of 4VL integrity features and operators. But SQL has only one NULL and will therefore produce erroneous 3VL answers.

❖ **Note:** For simplicity, the continuous *dropping* of variables at various points in time is ignored. Although such discontinuations further complicate the design, they do not affect the argument. The reader should consider the implications as an exercise.

10.3.2.2 NULLs and 3VL

Users can avoid inapplicable values in base tables via entity subtype-supertype designs (see Chapter 6). For example, the 1976 admission variables (the supertype attributes) would map to one table and the 1995 admission variable (the subtype attribute) to another.

```
ADM76 {ADM#,PAT_ID,CLASS,SPONSOR}
ADM95 {ADM#,THOSP_ID}
```

But even if users adhere to this 3VL discipline, a SQL DBMS will still generate NULLs for inapplicable values in derived tables, such as views and query results. An obvious case is the outer join operation and if the input tables to it are views and contain NULLs for missing (unknown) values, the outer join will generate NULLs for *both* missing and inapplicable values. If such results are then input to further manipulation, wrong answers will ensue [13]. Besides, such designs still suffer from the problems associated with 3VL (and any DBMS-specific implementation quirks thereof).

10.3.2.3 2VL and Metadata

Users could opt for the metadata approach to missing information. However, because no current DBMS supports it, the implementation would have to be manual.

First, each entity supertype and subtype would have to be mapped to as many tables as there are *combinations* of unknown attribute values. For a two-attribute entity subtype like '95 Admission', for example, the maximum possible combinations of missing values is two (key values cannot be missing). If any THOSP_ID values are missing, the design would be

```
ADM952 {ADM#,THOSP_ID}
ADM951 {ADM#}
```

For a five-attribute entity supertype like '1976 Admission', there are 15 different possible combinations of nonkey unknown values (4 one-attribute, 6 two-attribute, 3 three-attribute, and 1 four-attribute), so if all combinations actually occur, the maximum number of tables is 15, and so on for each entity type. It should be obvious that the number of possible combinations—and, thus, base tables—increases steeply with the number of attributes. For example, adding a sixth attribute increases the possible combinations from 15 to 36! Not all combinations do occur in real-world databases, but with hundreds of attributes, tables can proliferate, and many can have very few rows and/or columns.

Second, the appropriate metatables would have to be created and maintained by users, as well as the relationships among the data tables, and between them and the metatables (because current DBMSs do not have user-extendible catalogs, such tables would actually be user tables in practice).

Third, table operations would have to be modified to output multiple tables as shown in Figure 10.6.

The burden is prohibitive and prone to error. Besides, even this strategy cannot entirely eliminate NULLs because SQL DBMSs can still generate them.

> ❖ **Note:** Objections to the metadata approach are also likely to be made on performance grounds, namely that large numbers of tables increase the I/O load. But first, as one of the quotes at the beginning of this chapter indicates, the use of NULLs has its own performance drawbacks. Second, more tables do not necessarily translate into greater I/O and/or slow performance—this depends on many implementation aspects, such as the DBMS optimizer and its physical management capabilities, physical database design, hardware resources, user access patterns, and so on. Performance is a *physical* implementation issue, separate from any *logical* aspects, such as treatment of missing values.

It is precisely for these reasons that metadata management (definition, manipulation and integrity enforcement) is a *database function* and the province of the DBMS. It can be argued that, in principle, a

DBMS with direct and proper support of the metadata approach to missing values can be designed to handle any number of tables, relieving users from drudgery. Such a DBMS would, for example, provide facilities to create the related data tables and generate the pertinent metadata tables; transparently generate views combining the rows in the related data tables upon user data requests; and transparently update the data and metadata tables when missing data is updated by users. And its optimizer would, of course, address the performance implications. But all this is moot because the prospects of metadata support by the industry are practically nil.

10.4 Conclusion and Recommendations

It is very important to realize that the ultimate source of difficulties caused by missing information is not database technology per se, but rather imperfect knowledge of reality, which limits what can be asserted about the real world. No complications would arise if knowledge about the reality of interest were perfect, so the only real solution is zero tolerance for missing values in the database. Unfortunately, perfection is not achievable in practice, which imposes a choice between two alternatives, both of which have drawbacks

- Avoiding missing values by recording only assertions known to be true; this requires the DBMS to handle very large numbers of tables and intricate relationships between them.

- Allowing missing values in the database; this complicates the data language, reduces intuitiveness and interpretability of results, and practically guarantees incorrect answers.

> ❖ **Note:** A **default values** approach to missing information has also been proposed [14]. However, it does not get around the issue of bundling data with metadata. Because, like the metadata approach, it would require major surgery, it is unlikely that it will be implemented commercially.

The database industry has opted for the latter alternative and adopted SQL's NULLs. Vendors have, thus, avoided the intricacies of the metadata approach, but have exposed users to the perils of 3VL and its predictable implementation flaws. It is highly unlikely that SQL will be revised to support the metadata approach because aside from major surgery, the elimination of NULLs will render existing databases and applications invalid. Because manual implementation of the metadata approach is not practical for users, all that can be done is minimizing NULLs in base tables and exercising extreme care in formulating queries and interpreting results in the presence of NULLs (not an easy task either).

In this context, the burden of a manual metadata approach would at least provide a disincentive for the casual allowance of missing values in databases. SQL's way is more insidious because, in the absence of such a burden, users are lured into a false sense of security and are unlikely to be aware of wrong answers.

References

[1] Hugh Darwen, "The Duplicity of Duplicate Rows," *Relational Database Writings 1989–1991*, Reading, MA: Addison-Wesley, 1992.

[2] D. McGoveran, "Nothing from Nothing," Parts 1–4, *Relational Database Writings 1994–1997*, Reading, MA: Addison-Wesley, 1998.

[3] C. J. Date, "NOT Is Not 'Not'!" *Relational Database Writings 1985–1989*, Reading, MA: Addison-Wesley, 1990.

[4] C. J. Date, "Why Three-Valued Logic Is a Mistake," *Relational Database Writings 1991–1994*, Reading, MA: Addison-Wesley, 1995.

[5] C. J. Date, "Three-Valued Logic in the Real World," *Relational Database Writings 1989–1991*, Reading, MA: Addison-Wesley, 1992.

[6] C. J. Date et al., "Nothing to Do with the Case," *Relational Database Writings 1994–1997*, Reading, MA: Addison-Wesley, 1998.

[7] C. J. Date, "Up to a Point. Lord Copper," *Relational Database Writings 1994–1997*, Reading, MA: Addison-Wesley, 1998.

[8] C. J. Date, "Null Values in Database Management," *Relational Database Selected Writings*, Reading, MA: Addison-Wesley, 1986.

[9] C. J. Date, "A Note on the Logical Operators of SQL," *Relational Database Writings 1991–1994*, Reading, MA: Addison-Wesley, 1995.

[10] F. Pascal, *Understanding Relational Databases*, New York, NY: John Wiley & Sons, 1993.

[11] C. J. Date, *A Guide to the SQL Standard*, 4th ed., Reading, MA: Addison-Wesley, 1997.

[12] C. J. Date, "EXISTS Is Not 'Exists'!" *Relational Database Writings 1985–1989*, Reading, MA: Addison-Wesley, 1990.

[13] C. J. Date, "Watch Out for Outer Join" and "Outer Join with No Nulls and Fewer Tears," *Relational Database Writings 1989–1991*, Reading, MA: Addison-Wesley, 1992.

[14] C. J. Date, "Faults and Defaults," Parts 1–5, *Relational Database Writings 1994–1997*, Reading, MA: Addison-Wesley, 1998.

[15] C. J. Date, "Round and Round the Nullberry Bush," *Relational Database Writings 1994–1997*, Reading, MA: Addison-Wesley, 1998.

[16] C. J. Date, "Nothing in Excess," *Relational Database Writings 1991–1994*, Reading, MA: Addison-Wesley, 1995.

[17] C. J. Date, "Much Ado about Nothing," *Relational Database Writings 1991–1994*, Reading, MA: Addison-Wesley, 1995.

[18] H. Darwen, "Nothing Really Matters," *Relational Database Writings 1989–1991*, Reading, MA: Addison-Wesley, 1992.

[19] C. J. Date, "Oh No Not Nulls Again," *Relational Database Writings 1989–1991*, Reading, MA: Addison-Wesley, 1992.

[20] H. Warden, "Into the Unknown," *Relational Database Writings 1985–1989*, Reading, MA: Addison-Wesley, 1990.

Index